early

Communication Skills

early

Communication Skills

Charlotte Lynch & Julia Kidd

Speechmark

Please note that in this text 'he' is used to refer to the child for the sake of clarity alone.

Published by
Speechmark Publishing Ltd, Telford Road, Bicester, Oxon OX26 4LQ,
United Kingdom
www.speechmark.net

© Charlotte Lynch & Julia Kidd, 1999
First published in 1991
Second Edition 1999
Reprinted 2000, 2001

002-4208/Printed in the United Kingdom/1010

British Library Cataloguing in Publication Data
Lynch, Charlotte
Kidd, Julia
Early Communication Skills.— (Early Skills Series)
I. Title II. Series

ISBN 0 86388 373 7
(Previously published by Winslow Press Ltd under ISBN 0 86388 223 4)

EARLY COMMUNICATION SKILLS
Contents

ACKNOWLEDGEMENTS

This publication would not have been possible without the interest shown by colleagues, both in education and in health. We would particularly like to thank Gill Edelman, Morag Bowen and Terry Callaghan for their encouragement and support throughout. We are very grateful to David Eccles and Anna Cooper for their help with the resource pictures.

We are indebted to the parents and children with whom we have worked and hope that this publication will be of benefit to them and other parents.

PREFACE TO THE REVISED EDITION

In response to feedback from colleagues, this edition of *Early Communication Skills* has been made more user-friendly and includes a greater breadth of activities. The new format makes the activity pages easier to photocopy and brings it into line with the other books in this series. The new section on 'Language and Play' aims to extend some of the activities of the earlier edition, and add new ones, with an emphasis on maximizing language opportunities in the home.

After consultation with readers of the first edition, it was felt that the points in the manual could be incorporated into the photocopiable sheets. This has been done through a question and answer format, in the form of 'General Points', which aims to give readers a clearer understanding of the purpose of various activities, using as little jargon as possible. Record-keeping sheets have also been adapted, and recap the general aim of each section, in a simple but focused way.

Charlotte Lynch & Julia Kidd

INTRODUCTION

This book is aimed at the professional working with pre-school children and their parents, carers or teachers, and should be valuable in homes, playgroups and nurseries, providing a framework on which to base activities. It will be of particular interest to those new to this age group or entering the specialist area of hearing impairment.

BACKGROUND

The activities were originally developed from a collection of practical ideas and approaches used by a speech & language therapist and a teacher of the deaf working together in a Total Communication nursery (combining signing and aural approach). It has subsequently proved to be beneficial to other children with communication difficulties, and has been adapted and extended as a result of the interest shown by colleagues and parents.

The activities are based on the principle that all children learn best through play. In the authors' experience, many parents or carers of children with communication difficulties are looking for specific ideas which will encourage progress. Many of the activities in this book can be naturally incorporated into everyday routines and it is hoped that they will build on the skills which parents and carers already have in communicating with their children.

HOW TO USE THIS BOOK

The activities are divided into nine different sections for ease of use, and cover some of the prerequisite skills essential for future language development. These skills are all interrelated, and activities may be selected from different sections and worked on simultaneously, according to the individual needs of the child.

Each set of activities is preceded by 'General Points', which provide the rationale for the particular activities. Targets can be discussed and agreed jointly by professional and parent or carer, using the tick boxes at the side of each activity to plan and record activities carried out. Parents, carers or key workers can be further involved in joint assessment through the record sheet at the end of each section, or through additional records of progress in *Early Listening*, *Vocalizations* and *Early Words*. These may be particularly useful for parents/carers who will observe their child in many different settings over a long period of time.

The activity sheets can be photocopied, and are intended to be distributed to parents/carers or other key workers at the discretion of the teacher or therapist, following explanation and demonstration where appropriate. They may be used in the home with parents, childminders or other main carers, and in playgroups, crèches and nurseries.

SELECTING ACTIVITIES

Activities within each section are in approximate developmental order. The rate of children's development across and within different skills, however, does not necessarily follow the same pattern, so no age guide is given. Although the majority of activities were written with the under-fives in mind, some will be suitable for older children. Selection of activities and materials will be dependent on the professional judgement of those working with individual children and their families.

It will be important to bear in mind the setting in which activities will be carried out. Some activities might be more appropriate in a clinical or school setting. Others will be more easily carried out in the home environment. *Pre-verbal Skills* and *Language & Play* focus on a natural approach to communication, which it is hoped many parents/carers will feel comfortable with. Many of the suggested activities do not require special teaching skills, allowing parents/carers and other key workers to develop their own natural style.

Other sections, such as *Speech Discrimination*, are more formal and complex, and will require more guidance from the speech & language therapist, if they are to be carried out in different settings. More detailed explanations of these activities for the therapist or the teacher can be found at the beginning of this section. Selection of words or sounds used in these activities should always be made in consultation with the professionals concerned. Photocopiable resource pictures for use with syllable discrimination and minimal pairs are at the end of the section.

Several activities from one section may be carried out simultaneously in different settings, all working towards the same goal. In *Early Listening (Awareness of Voice)*, for example, the family might focus on 'Symbolic Sounds' (p50), the speech and language therapist could work in a more formal setting with 'Voice/no voice' activities (p54) while the teacher might try 'Listening for words and sounds' (p52).

When working with children who have a hearing loss, it will be necessary to consider whether the materials suggested are within the child's range of hearing. Most of the materials suggested in this book are available in every household. The resources list at the end of the book suggests alternative specialist equipment for the listening activities which may be more suitable for use with the profoundly or severely deaf.

HINTS FOR PARENTS

Play

1 Everyday activities provide the best opportunities for learning language. Talk to your child about what you are doing throughout the day and try to involve him where possible.

2 Try to set aside some time during the day for play activities when you can give your attention to your child. This could be part of a routine which your child looks forward to, perhaps after a drink or a nap when he is not tired or hungry. Choose a time that suits you as well as your child. It is important for you to feel alert and relaxed too.

3 If you have more than one child, it is important that they learn to play together. A child with communication difficulties, however, may be very demanding, and may respond better to some individual attention if this is possible. Try to arrange to spend some time together when other children are asleep or out of the house.

4 Two short play sessions of about 10–15 minutes may suit your child better than one long one.

5 Get down to your child's level where he can see and hear you best.

6 Keep some special toys aside for play sessions.

7 Try to put toys away which are not being used. Too many toys are distracting.

8 Switch off the television when playing with your child. Background noise or music can be particularly distracting for a child with a hearing loss.

9 Children learn best when they are interested in something. Follow your child's own interests and ideas. Don't worry if your child does not want to do what you had planned.

10 If your child shows signs of becoming fed up with an activity, leave it and come back to it later, before you both end up getting frustrated.

Improving Communication

It may be helpful to think about the answers to some of the following questions if you are looking for ways of improving communication. Most of the questions are also relevant to those using sign language. Do you:

◆ Give your child time to talk (or sign)?

◆ Make sure you have your child's attention before you speak (or sign)?

◆ Try not to speak too fast?

◆ Give your child lots of praise?

◆ Make sure you are in a position where your child can see you?

◆ Follow your child's lead in play?

◆ Comment on what your child is looking at or doing?

◆ Repeat and expand on what your child says?

◆ Think about your lip patterns?

◆ Use intonation and facial expression to help with communication?

◆ Rephrase what you are saying if your child has not heard or understood?

PRE-VERBAL SKILLS

Pre-Verbal Skills
EYE CONTACT

General points

What is meant by 'eye contact' and why is it important?

Communication between two people involves looking at each other and making eye contact, as well as talking. Establishing and maintaining good eye contact is an important social skill. Looking at the speaker's face will also provide information about language through facial expression, gestures, lip patterns and signs.

Very young children with communication difficulties may only make fleeting eye contact. This may cause communication to break down, as parents may get the message that the child is not interested.

Looking together at things in the environment is another important part of communication. The child looks at an object, the parent follows his gaze and makes a comment. This is the beginning of conversations and turn taking. Children with a hearing loss, however, may not be able to make sense of what the parent says, so these early communication skills may not develop easily.

How can eye contact be improved?

You may need to practise your own facial expressions, to make them more interesting to look at. Emotions and feelings such as being happy, sad, angry or tired can all be exaggerated. When your child looks at you, use the opportunity to make a funny face, or show him something interesting. Holding objects near the face and making them disappear behind the head is one way of encouraging children to look at the speaker's face.

There are plenty of opportunities for improving eye contact throughout the day: for example, waiting a second before giving your child a drink, although it is important to avoid battles over this. Encouraging eye contact should be as natural as possible. You do not need to move your child's face towards you. Children will look when *they* want to.

Pre-Verbal Skills
EYE CONTACT

❑ **Tracking**

Your child will learn to follow toys with his eyes. Balloons, bubbles and puppets on a stick are interesting to watch.

Your child may watch your face while you are blowing up balloons or blowing bubbles. Blow up balloons slowly. Wait for eye contact between each breath.

Make puppets or wooden spoon faces disappear behind your face and wait for eye contact.

❑ **Party blowers**

Blowing party horns will encourage your child to watch what you are doing.

❑ **Coloured feathers**

Blow feathers at your child and tickle him with the feathers.

❑ **Noisy toys**

Squeaky toys, rattles, bells or whistles can be used to encourage eye contact. Choose a toy and make a noise. Stop the noise and wait for eye contact before you start again.

❑ **Hiding games**

Wave a coloured scarf up and down over your child so that he can feel the breeze. Lift it high and let it fall over your head. Encourage your child to pull it off your head.

❑ **Peepo games**

Peepo games can be played from behind the furniture, the curtains, or when getting dressed.

❑ Face masks

Make face masks from paper plates and cut out holes for eyes, nose and mouth. Use the mask to play peepo or 'boo' games.

❑ Silver cake cases

Try to attract your child's attention by putting silver cake cases over your eyes and playing peepo games.

❑ Sunglasses

Try putting dark sunglasses on and off to encourage your child to look at you.

❑ Binoculars

Look through two old toilet roll tubes to encourage eye contact. Longer kitchen roll tubes can be used for telescopes. Decorating them with coloured paper will make them more attractive to look at.

❑ Hand games

Wave your hands and wiggle your fingers. Hide your face behind your hands and play peepo games. Draw faces on your fingers or use finger puppets. Wiggle them near your face and hide them.

❑ Hats/wigs

Put hats on and off or hide your face behind a hat and play peepo games. Real or play wigs can be used in the same way.

❑ Songs and rhymes

Pat-a-cake clapping games, round-and-round-the-garden tickling games and row-the-boat rocking games are all useful for improving eye contact. Stop singing occasionally and wait for eye contact before continuing.

❑ Ball games

When playing games of throw and catch, wait for your child to look at you before throwing the ball, or hide it behind your back until you get eye contact. If your child is not looking, do something silly like putting it on your head or up your jumper. Instead of using balls, you can use bean bags, rubber rings or hoops.

❏ *Wink games/pass on faces*

Play winking games or make funny faces for your child to copy.

❏ *Face paints*

Using face paints, paint faces on your child's face and on your own face. Make clown faces, animal faces, pirate faces.

NB Some children may be reluctant to have faces drawn on them until they are older.

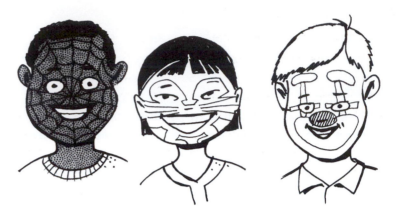

Pre-Verbal Skills
ATTENTION

General points

What is meant by 'attention' and why is it important?

It is not unusual for young children to have a short span of attention. Working on 'attention' aims to extend the time a child is able to concentrate on, or 'attend to', one activity. Improving concentration will be helpful in all areas of learning. A good attention span will help children understand language more easily.

As children become more mature, their level of attention changes. For example, a typical one-year-old is easily distracted. The typical two-year-old may have very definite ideas about how to play, and will be resistant to adult intervention. By the age of three, children become more flexible in their play, and can begin to give their attention to adult instructions. Some children may need help to move from one stage of attention to the next.

How can attention span be improved?

◆ It is helpful to remove distractions.

◆ Choose toys or materials which your child is most interested in.

◆ Playing with the same object in many different ways can help to develop attention span.

◆ Adding surprise to games will help add to enjoyment and interest; for example, hiding things or wrapping them in paper.

◆ Most importantly, follow your child's lead. It may be enough simply to play alongside your child, showing an interest and commenting on what he is doing.

◆ As your child's attention span improves, encouraging eye contact and allowing him time to respond to your suggestions will be helpful.

❑ Balloons

Blow them up and let them go.

Feel the air coming out of them.

Make appropriate noises: wheee! whoosh!

Throw them and catch them.

Bounce them.

Draw faces on them.

Stick shapes on them.

Half-fill them with coloured water and freeze them.

Glue newspaper on them to make papier mâché models, and paint them.

Pop them!

❑ Nesting barrels or stacking beakers

Use them for counting and matching colours.

Build towers in different ways.

Roll them to each other.

Hide things inside them and play memory games.

Sort coloured sweets into them.

Play with them in the bath; fill them with water or float them.

Use them to make sandcastles.

Wash them.

Hide them around the room.

❑ Coloured beads, buttons or cotton reels

Make necklaces, bracelets or 'snakes'.

Sort them into colours, shapes and sizes.

Put them in pots and shake them.

Make patterns, such as red–blue–red–blue.

Make towers.

Hide them in your pockets.

❑ *Feely boxes*

Have an object of interest in the box and open the lid slowly. Let your child put his hand in the box and feel it. Then take the object out and play with it. Objects of interest could include the following:

◆ a glove puppet give it a 'pretend' drink
give it a kiss
give it a hat
stroke the puppet
(more ideas in *Vocalizations*, p59,
encouraging babble)

◆ an apple   wash it
cut it into halves/quarters
count the pips
peel it
make apple sauce
make apple pie
plant the pips

◆ playdough   roll it out and cut out shapes with
pastry cutters
make balls or sausages
make models: cats, snakes, birthday
cakes with 'candles', snowmen, bird's
nest with eggs in it, bracelets, rings,
watches

◆ a bean bag   throw it and catch it
shake it
balance it on the head
hide it
throw it into a box or basket

❏ *Inset puzzles*

Take all the pieces out and put them back in. As you are doing this, talk about each piece and learn the words or signs.

Hide one piece and ask your child which one is missing; or hide a piece in one hand and let your child guess which hand it is in.

Match puzzle pieces to real objects.

Put pieces in empty pots and shake them.

Draw round them.

Make them stand up.

❏ *Toy bricks*

Build towers or walls and knock them down.

Line the bricks up and push them along a table, like a train.

Play peepo games with them.

Bang them together.

Hide bricks of different colours or sizes around the room. Play 'Hunt the matching brick'.

Wooden bricks of different shapes can be made into simple animal shapes: for example, cats or giraffes.

Make squares or rectangles with them.

Make patterns: for example, big–small–big–small.

❏ *Posting boxes*

As well as posting shapes into them, try playing with the shapes in unusual ways, to make it more of a social game; for example:

hide one behind your back or in one of your hands,

put one on your head,

hide one in your pocket/down your jumper/up your sleeve,

throw one and catch it,

draw round the shapes and colour them,

make towers with them.

❏ Books and songs

Lift-the-flap books, pop-up books, musical books and 'feely books' may be more interesting for your child, holding his attention longer. Singing rhymes and songs with actions over and over again helps children to anticipate what comes next.

Simple dressing up may make singing more exciting. A driver's hat could be worn to accompany 'The wheels on the bus go round and round'. Finger puppets or small playdough models can be made for familiar rhymes: 'Two little dicky birds'; 'Five fat sausages', 'Five currant buns', 'Five little ducks', 'Humpty Dumpty', and so on.

❏ Drawing pictures

Drawing pictures of well-known songs, stories or favourite toys can help keep children interested. 'Humpty Dumpty', 'Twinkle, twinkle, little star' and the 'Gingerbread Man' are quite easy to draw. Sing the words while you are drawing and colouring in.

Draw pictures of houses, buses, cars or tractors with pictures or photographs of your child and other people looking out of the window.

Draw simple face pictures: suns, flowers and stars can have faces as well as people and animals.

Pre-Verbal Skills
BREATH CONTROL
General points

What is meant by 'breath control' and why is it important?

Good breath control is important for the production of speech. When we speak, we control the use of our breath in a very complex way. This has been practised and perfected from very early on, through the experimental babble that young babies and children make. Children with severe hearing loss may draw their breath in for speech, rather than breathe it out, as they have difficulty matching the sounds they make with those around them. Children with cerebral palsy or cleft palate may have poor control over the muscles used for speech.

How can breath control be improved?

There are many blowing games which can be used to help improve breath control. Blowing on the skin, blowing hair or blowing steam on the mirror or windows can help young children become aware of breath, by feeling and seeing it. At first children may just watch. Later, they may try to copy.

Pre-Verbal Skills
BREATH CONTROL

❑ **Blowing games**

Blow bubbles off the surface of soapy water.

Blow bubbles off toys or off hands at bathtime.

Blow talcum powder off hands.

Blow feathers.

Blow mobiles.

Blow boats or plastic ducks on the water.

Blow tissue paper fish.

❑ **Harder blowing games**

Blow ping pong balls.

Blow bubbles in the water, through thick and thin straws, starting with thick straws, which are easier to blow through.

Blow windmills.

Blow out candles.

Blow paper horns.

Blow bubbles through a ring.

Blow party whistles.

Blow small toys off the edge of the bath.

Blow paint across a piece of paper, with or without a straw.

Blow mouth organs/toy trumpets/recorders.

Practise long breaths and short breaths.

Pre-Verbal Skills
COPYING

General points

Why is copying important in the development of communication skills?

Copying is an important skill to learn as it involves co-operation and interaction between two people, which is necessary for communication.

Children learn language by copying what they hear and see. Early communication between parent and child begins with the parent copying sounds or faces the child makes and making them meaningful. Games which encourage copying should help to improve observation and imitation skills which will be important for the learning of speech or signs.

How can copying be improved?

Join in with your child's play, and encourage him to copy what you do too. Copy your child's noises, gestures and facial expressions, and extend them to make them meaningful.

There will be times when children are too engrossed in their own play to copy what you are doing, but playing alongside your child will help to extend his own ideas.

Provide opportunities for your child to copy your everyday routines, for example letting him have a cloth to help you wipe the table.

Pre-Verbal Skills
COPYING

EARLY COPYING

❑ ***Toy bricks***

Start by copying what your child does. For example, if he bangs two bricks together, you do the same. If he has difficulty, take his hands and help him bang them together. Then try to extend the play and see if your child copies: for example, lift the bricks high in the air and bang them together.

❑ ***Early pretend play***

First copy your child's play. If he puts a hat on, you do the same with the other one. Later, see if your child will copy your actions, for example drinking from a 'pretend' cup or putting sunglasses on.

❑ ***Copying faces and sounds***

Make funny faces in the mirror and encourage your child to copy you. Copy any faces he makes.

Make funny sounds. Vowel sounds and babble, such as ahhhh/oo, ma-ma-ma/ba-ba-ba, are the easiest to start with.

Copying sounds should not be too formal. Try to find sounds or faces which amuse your child. Respond to any sounds your child makes and copy them.

You will need:

two plastic cups
two hats
two pairs of sunglasses

oooO!

❑ ***Dolls and teddies***

There are many ways of encouraging copying by playing with dolls and teddies. You could have a doll or teddy each, or play with the same one together.

Pretend to feed them and give them a drink.

Make them jump, run or turn somersaults.

Dress, undress them and put them to bed.

Wash them and brush their teeth.

Give them a bath.

Give them a kiss/hug.

Sit them on a toy car.

Hide them.

❑ *Small rubber ring or plastic rings on a stick*

Roll the ring.

Spin it round.

Balance it on your head.

Put it round your wrist/arm/ankle/feet.

Pretend it is a steering wheel and that you are driving a car.

❑ *Beads, pegs and bricks*

Copy patterns (red–blue–red–blue).

Copy towers or bridges.

Match shapes and colours.

Copy patterns and shapes in a peg board.

Copy simple *Lego*® or *Duplo*® models.

COPYING ACTIONS

❑ *'Simon says' games*

Encourage copying of actions, for example:

Simon says, "Clap your hands."
Simon says, "Wave your hands."
Simon says, "Shake your head."
Simon says, "Touch your nose."
Simon says, "Put out your tongue."

Join in the actions as you say them so that your child can copy you.

❑ *Follow my leader*

This game will be easier with more than one child, in a large space. Everyone follows the leader's actions, for example:

marching,
hopping,
jumping,
walking with hands on head.

Children could march round with a musical instrument.

❑ *Songs and rhymes*

Sing songs and action rhymes which encourage copying:

'Here we go round the mulberry bush',
'Ring a ring o' roses',
'Wind the bobbin up',
'The wheels on the bus go round and round'.

Pre-Verbal Skills
TURN TAKING
General points

Why is learning to take turns important for communication?

Communication involves listening, waiting and taking turns. Two people having a conversation take turns to speak, gesture and make eye contact. If two people talk at once, communication breaks down.

Turn taking begins very early, long before children learn to talk. Parents respond to sounds which their baby makes, and the baby repeats the sound again, resulting in a 'conversation' where the two speakers listen to each other and take their turn.

It should be encouraged early on to help develop an understanding of the rules of conversational turn taking as well as encouraging good behaviour.

How can turn taking be improved?

Many young children find it difficult to learn to share, wait and take turns. These skills should be encouraged early on, to develop an understanding of the rules of conversational turn taking as well as promoting good standards of behaviour. The rules of turn taking and sharing must be clear and firm.

Turn taking can be encouraged throughout the day. To begin with, encourage turn taking when you are alone with your child. It is much harder for young children to share with brothers, sisters and friends of a similar age.

Your child must understand the language (either signed or spoken) for turn taking: for example, my turn/your turn. If your child is reluctant to take turns, let him have two turns for every one you have. Give lots of praise when your child has shared well and waited for a turn. Encourage children to thank each other for taking turns.

EVERYDAY SHARING

Children can be helped to understand about taking turns by:

using an egg timer – children can see how long their turn is;
clock timer – which can be set for a short period of time;
being prepared to give up a toy after a count to 10.

There are many opportunities to encourage turn taking and sharing during everyday routines, particularly if there are brothers and sisters, although this may not always be easy!

❏ *Cooking*

Take turns to stir cake mixture.

Take turns to sieve the flour.

Take turns to cut the pastry (encourage children to work together and help each other: one could cut the shapes and the other could put them into tins).

❏ *Gardening*

Plant seeds or pips. Children can take turns with different 'jobs': one can put soil into pots, the other can plant the seeds or add some water.

Sweep leaves: one child can sweep with a broom or brush and the other can collect the leaves into a bag or bucket.

EARLY TURN TAKING

If your child is reluctant to give up one toy, offer him another one, and let him have it only when the first one is returned. This helps your child to learn how to give and take.

❏ **Balls and bean bags**

Sit opposite your child and throw balls or bean bags to each other. Try this with brothers, sisters and friends.

❏ **Wind-up toys or cars**

Send wind-up toys backwards and forwards to each other across a table, or take turns to roll cars towards each other.

❏ **Posting boxes**

Take turns to post a shape in the box.

❏ **Skittles and ball**

Take turns to roll the ball and knock down the skittles.

❏ **Pop-up toys**

Take turns to press the button to make Jack-in-the-box jump up or a pop-up rocket take off.

❏ **Rings on a stick**

Take turns to put the next ring on the stick. You could pretend to put the wrong one on.

❏ **Lift-the-flap books**

Take turns to lift the flap. Remind children whose turn it is next before you turn the page.

❏ **Building beakers or bricks**

Take turns to add another beaker or brick to a tower. Praise children for helping each other.

❏ **Fishing games**

Take turns to 'catch a fish', using a magnet at the end of a fishing line. Let each child collect their fish in a small container.

❏ **Puppets**

Teach a 'naughty' puppet to share and take turns, and say "please" and "thank you".

❏ **Bubble gun**

Take it in turns to make bubbles. If children are reluctant to part with the toy after just one go, they could each have two or three goes.

❏ **Board games**

Games such as Lotto can encourage turn taking. Lotto games can be made at home, using photographs of family and friends.

Taking turns to throw the dice in board games may be helpful. Shape or colour matching dice will be easier to start with.

Pre-Verbal Skills
RECORD SHEET

Child's name: ....

Pre-verbal skills are essential for establishing a foundation on which to build future speech and language.

AIM OF ACTIVITIES	COMMENT AND DATE
To improve **EYE CONTACT (p3).** This is an important social skill and will provide information about language.	
Activities tried:	
To improve **ATTENTION (p7)**. This is important to support the learning process.	
Activities tried:	
To promote appropriate **BREATH CONTROL (p12)**. This is important for the production of speech.	
Activities tried:	
To encourage **COPYING (p14)**. This is important for social interaction and the learning of language.	
Activities tried:	
To develop **TURN TAKING (p17)**. This is important in social interaction and conversation.	
Activities tried:	

LANGUAGE & PLAY

Language & Play

General points

WHY IS PLAY IMPORTANT?

Play is important for language development and imaginative thinking. There are tremendous opportunities for language developments through different types of play.

Exploratory play

Through play with toys and everyday objects, babies discover that they can make things happen. For example, when they shake a rattle it makes a noise. In the same way, when they make a noise, they are quite likely to get some attention.

Providing a wide range of household objects as well as toys for children to explore will help them to learn about shapes, sounds, colours and textures. In the early stages, they will learn by shaking, banging, dropping and looking at things and putting them in their mouths. As children discover the similarities and differences between objects, they also learn that different things have names.

It may be a while before children say any words, but exploration of toys and objects provides them with the experience they will need to understand language. At a later stage, exploring different objects and materials is useful in developing an understanding of more complex vocabulary.

Physical play

Physical play and rough-and-tumble games will give your child experience of movement and space. This will help him develop an understanding of the meaning of action words (throw, kick, run, jump and so on) and prepositions (in order of difficulty: up, down, on, in, under, through, between, behind, in front, and so on).

Everyday experiences

Children learn by experiencing different situations. Real experiences and everyday routines are very important for the development of children's imaginary play and language.

Symbolic play

All words (whether signed or spoken) are symbols. Children have to be able to think in symbols before they can make sense of language. Pretending to give a doll, teddy or person a drink from a cup is one of the first steps of symbolic play. At a later stage, symbolic play offers opportunities to extend more complex vocabulary.

Co-operative play

Learning to play together is an essential part of early communication. Children learn language and social skills from each other and spark off imaginative ideas in play.

Imaginative and role play

Children who play 'shops' are learning about the world by acting out their own experiences. They are also experimenting with language and communication. Children whose speech and language are delayed will still need activities appropriate to their age and interest. They may play imaginatively, but need help in communicating their ideas through speech or sign.

Free play

It is also important for children to have time to play on their own, and to 'talk to themselves'. This gives them a chance to experiment with sounds and language. Younger children may babble to themselves, and enjoy listening to the sounds they make. This type of sound play is not intended for communication, but helps children to work out sound patterns in their brain.

❏ *Using the senses*

Give your child experience of lots of different things to play with. A collection of safe household objects and ordinary materials are interesting for young children. Collect items such as:

wooden/metal spoons	plastic/paper plates
shiny paper	tissue paper
cellophane	newspaper
ribbons	headscarves
old tights	empty pots/biscuit tins
wool	old set of keys
bells	cotton reels
scraps of different materials	old kitchen/toilet roll tubes
baby brush	jam jar/coffee lids
plastic bottles	

◆ Have a special box or basket for household objects which are safe for your child, and change the contents regularly so that your child does not lose interest.

◆ Put the objects in feely boxes or drawstring bags and take out one at a time to explore.

◆ Crumple up or tear bits of paper to make noises.

◆ Bang things together and take them in and out of empty pots with lids on.

◆ Cover things with a scarf and encourage your child to pull it off.

◆ Stuff old tights with wool or other objects.

◆ Fasten ribbons to old kitchen roll tubes and wave them.

◆ Make a wooden spoon puppet pop up and down a cardboard tube.

◆ Make things disappear down tubes.

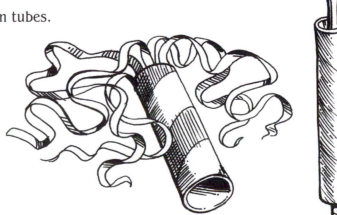

Many actions and words can be explored in the following games:

❑ ### Ball play

Throw, **catch** and **kick** a ball (high, low, up, down).

Throw it **into** a bucket **through** a hoop/basketball net.

Roll it **down** a slide.

Throw it **over** a wall/fence.

Roll it **through** your legs.

Bounce it on the ground.

Hit it with a tennis racket.

Kick it **under** a chair.

Roll it **through** a tunnel.

❑ ### Boxes

Climb **in** and **out** of boxes.

Open each end of a large box to make a tunnel to climb **through**.

Make a house with a door to go **in** and **out** of.

Throw things **into** boxes.

Jump over small boxes.

Run round a line of boxes.

❑ ### Hide and seek

Hide **behind** the door, **under** the table, **in** the bed, and so on.

Hide things **under** the cushions, **in** a box, **behind** the curtains, **on** the cupboard, and so on.

Language & Play
EVERYDAY EXPERIENCES

What you may see as work is like play to a young child. Always try to involve your child in everyday routines, even though this may mean your work does not get finished as quickly. It will be valuable experience for your child.

Helping with the washing
◆ Children can help collect dirty washing,
◆ remove sheets from beds,
◆ help load/unload the washing machine,
◆ pass the pegs when you hang the washing out to dry,
◆ put dry washing into a basket when you take it off the line,
◆ sort out the clothes and put them into cupboards.

Helping with certain cooking preparations
◆ Adding chopped sausages/sweetcorn/pineapple to pizzas,
◆ scrubbing potatoes,
◆ shelling peas,
◆ peeling sprouts (even if they don't like eating them!),
◆ shelling hard-boiled eggs,
◆ grating cheese,
◆ making fruit salad, jelly or sandwiches.

Younger children may like their own saucepan and spoon to 'pretend cook' while you are making the dinner, or they could wash up, using plastic pots, if you are prepared for wet floors!

❑ **Shopping**

On a visit to the local shop, your child could buy a small item, such as a magazine or a packet of crisps. Try to make sure he knows what he is going to buy at the shop, by drawing a picture if necessary before you go.

In the supermarket, children can help to carry certain items, put them in trolleys, help to unload the trolley and pack the bags, unpack the bags at home and help put the shopping away.

You could make a shopping list with pictures or labels of some items for your child to look out for.

❑ Outdoor activities

Children will enjoy helping to:
- ◆ wash their own toys
- ◆ wash wellington boots
- ◆ sweep up leaves
- ◆ take bottles to the bottle bank
- ◆ post letters
- ◆ plant seeds and flowers
- ◆ water the garden

❑ Bus journeys

Even if you do not usually take the bus, this will be an interesting experience for your child. Explain what you are going to do beforehand. Give your child the bus fare and let him look after the ticket on the journey. Save the ticket to stick in a diary or scrapbook when you get home, with a picture of a bus.

❑ Diaries

Keeping a simple diary of everyday experiences will help reinforce the language you have used with your child. Draw a picture of one thing you have enjoyed doing together each day, and write a short sentence underneath. You do not have to be a brilliant artist. Children only need a simple outline.

This sort of diary will be useful for communicating with your child about things which happened in the past.

❑ Photo book

Children with speech or language delay may have difficulty understanding where they are going when they get in a car or get dressed to go out. This can cause problems when they think they are going to the park, but end up in the supermarket.

A book of photographs can help to make communication easier with your child. This could include important people and places you are likely to visit:
- ◆ a photo of all the family members, including grand-parents/aunts/uncles;
- ◆ photos of important people in your child's life: child-minders/playgroup leaders/nursery teachers/friends/neighbours;
- ◆ photos of park/shops/playgroup/nursery/hospital/swimming pool.

Showing your child a photograph of the person or place you are going to visit before you leave the house will help him to anticipate what is going to happen next, until he understands the sign or the spoken word.

Language & Play
SYMBOLIC PLAY

❏ *Matching objects*

You will need a collection of familiar objects, including two identical objects (such as two cups). See if your child can find the two matching objects. If he can do this, match real objects to toy objects (for example, real cup and toy cup).

❏ *Matching objects to pictures*

Look at the book together and find the objects around the house to match the pictures. Or match a collection of objects to picture cards.

❏ *Tea parties*

Plastic tea sets are useful for 'pretend' parties, but not essential.

◆ Stick magazine pictures of food onto paper plates.
◆ Have a tea party with real or 'pretend' food.
◆ Let your child offer real or 'pretend' food to everyone in the family.
◆ Have a teddy bears' picnic in the house or outside.

You will need:

a first picture book with one picture on each page or picture cards; objects to match the pictures.

❏ *Large doll play*

Using dolls or teddies, pretend to:

◆ dress them, wash them and feed them;
◆ wash their clothes and hang them out to dry;
◆ take them for a walk in a toy pram or pushchair;
◆ make a bed from a cardboard box.

❑ Miniature toy play

Dolls' house and furniture

◆ Match the toy furniture to real furniture.
◆ Match the dolls to pictures or photographs of the family.
◆ Cut out catalogue pictures of furniture and stick them in a scrapbook.
◆ Make a house from four old shoe boxes. Sort the toy furniture into different rooms.
◆ Make the dolls go to sleep/wake up, "good morning"/"night night".
◆ Give them 'pretend' food.
◆ Brush their hair/dress/undress them.
◆ Give them a bath.

Zoo animals

◆ Make animal enclosures from *Duplo®*/*Lego®* bricks.
◆ Make 'pretend' rocks, caves or rivers with coloured bricks.
◆ Give animals a ride on a toy train.
◆ Put them on a boat in the water, or wash them at bathtime.
◆ Feed the animals 'pretend' food (play matching the food to the animal).
◆ Make kangaroos jump, penguins waddle, monkeys climb, seals swim, bears growl, lions roar.
◆ Sort animals into groups.
◆ Match them to pictures.
◆ Draw them.

❑ Farm animals

◆ Match the animals to pictures.
◆ Sort the animals into families.
◆ Learn the animal sounds, such as 'moo' and 'woof woof'.
◆ Hide the animals around the room or in your hand.
◆ Make the animals jump or run.
◆ Give them a ride in a tractor or trailer.

Ducks or hens: use a small box or basket for a nest and put 'pretend' eggs in it (*Lego®* bricks will do, or small chocolate eggs). Sing 'Five little ducks'.

Horses: build stables, fields or fences using bricks. They only have to be a simple square of bricks. Make a horse jump over the fence, and give a small doll or teddy a ride. Sing 'Horsey, horsey, don't you stop'.

Pigs: an empty matchbox can be a 'pretend' trough for the pig to eat out of. Make a pigsty using bricks or an old box. Give the pig a wash and make it go to sleep. Say the rhyme, 'This little piggy went to market'.

Cows: make a toy cow eat grass. Pretend the cow has lost her baby calf. Sing 'Hey diddle diddle' and pretend to make the cow jump over the moon.

Sheep: make up a story about a sheep in a field who escapes through a gap in the fence, and meets all the other animals. Sing 'Baa baa, black sheep'.

Make the animals talk to each other: for example, 'Hello/Bye bye/What's your name?'

❏ *Helping each other*

Doing a floor puzzle together.

Building a tower together with large bricks or *Lego*®.

Threading beads to make a necklace; one can choose the beads while the other threads them.

Making 'pretend' cakes/food with playdough or *Plasticine* to cook in a 'pretend' oven for a party. One child rolls out, the other puts in tins and then in the oven. Others can set the table for the party.

Sand and water play: one child can hold a funnel in a bottle while the other pours in sand or water.

One child can hold a basket or bucket, while the other tidies up bricks or toys.

❏ *Painting, colouring or gluing*

Children can help each other make large models or pictures:
- ◆ painting a large box together,
- ◆ making potato prints or fingerprints on a long piece of paper,
- ◆ covering a large box with scraps of tissue paper,
- ◆ colouring in a large picture.

❏ *Marble game*

Fix an old cardboard kitchen roll to the table with *Sellotape*. One child can roll marbles through the tube. The other can catch the marbles in a pot as they roll out of the tube and off the table at the other end.

> CARE MUST BE TAKEN WITH YOUNG CHILDREN TO ENSURE THAT THEY DO NOT PUT MARBLES INTO THEIR MOUTHS

Language & Play
IMAGINATIVE & ROLE PLAY

❑ *Boxes*

Collect large boxes for your child to climb in and out of. Boxes can become houses, boats, trains, cars, rockets and anything else your child wants them to be.

❑ *Chairs and tables*

Chairs lined up one behind the other can be trains. Simple 'tickets' and 'flags' can be made from scraps of paper. Children can have drinks and a snack in the 'buffet car'.

Houses or dens can be made using chairs, tables, pillows and blankets. They can also be boat cabins, buses or train carriages.

❑ *Shops*

A small table or upside-down box will make a good counter.

Make an OPEN/CLOSED sign and take it in turns to be the customer and the shopkeeper.

Act out the song, 'Five currant buns in a baker's shop', using cardboard cut-outs, real buns or simply bricks for 'pretend' buns. Favourite toys can buy a bun too.

Children can act out hospitals, hairdressers or cafes in similar ways.

❑ *Songs and stories*

Children can dress up as characters in well known songs and stories and act them out: 'There was a princess long ago', 'Old Roger is dead', 'Jack and Jill went up the hill', 'Ride a cock horse', 'Humpty Dumpty' and so on.

Language & Play
RECORD SHEET

Child's name: ....

Play is important for language development and imaginative thinking.

AIM OF ACTIVITIES	COMMENT AND DATE
EXPLORATORY PLAY (p25). To provide experience of a variety of materials using all the senses.	
Activities tried:	
PHYSICAL PLAY (p26). To develop understanding of vocabulary linked to movement and space.	
Activities tried:	
EVERYDAY EXPERIENCES (p27). To experience a variety of everyday routines.	
Activities tried:	
SYMBOLIC PLAY (p29). To realize that one object can represent another, and at a later stage to elaborate and extend children's language.	
Activities tried:	

AIM OF ACTIVITIES	COMMENT AND DATE
CO-OPERATIVE PLAY (p32). To develop language and social skills.	
Activities tried:	
IMAGINATIVE & ROLE PLAY (p33). To experiment with language and communication by acting out different scenarios.	
Activities tried:	

EARLY LISTENING: AWARENESS OF SOUND

SECTION 3

Early Listening: Awareness of Sound

General points

What is meant by 'awareness of sound' and why is it important?

Before children can understand the complex sounds of speech and language, they need to develop an awareness of sounds around them. Through exploration of a variety of different objects, children gradually learn to connect sounds to different actions and objects.

Babies are normally most interested in the sound of the human voice. For children with a severe or profound hearing loss, however, this may not be the case in the early stages. They may first need to understand that sound exists, and may feel the vibrations through the body before they are aware of sound through the ears.

How can awareness of sound be improved?

Introduce the word or sign for noisy and quiet. If your child makes a loud noise during play, cover your ears or make a sign to show that it is noisy.

Draw attention to things in your child's environment which can be both heard and felt, such as the washing machine, or music coming out of speakers. Give your child lots of experience of different sounds and vibrations.

Listening to sounds around you can be a part of everything you do together. Point out noises around and outside the house, for example:

◆ doors banging
◆ telephone ringing
◆ doorbell ringing
◆ running water
◆ traffic
◆ pneumatic drills
◆ dogs barking
◆ birds singing

Early Listening: Awareness of Sound
EXPLORING SOUND

Provide lots of experience of different sounds and vibrations.

❑ Things to bang

Wooden spoons/saucepan lids and metal spoons

Old jam pot lids/empty biscuit tins

Toy drum/tambourine

Put 'hundreds and thousands' on top of a biscuit tin and watch them moving as you bang on the tin. Try other small objects such as buttons or small pieces of tissue paper.

❑ Things to blow

Whistles/mouth organs/musical balloons/recorders/
toy trumpets

Musical balloons make a sound as the air comes out. Let your child feel the air coming out of the blower at the same time as hearing the sound.

❑ Things to shake

Sound shakers can be made by putting small objects inside old pots or tins, and shaking them to make a noise. These can be felt as well as heard. Rice, lentils and dried peas or pasta may be used if tins are firmly sealed with *Sellotape*. Tins filled with screw-on bottle tops and corks will make different sounds. Plastic containers will allow your child to see the movement inside as well as feel it.

You could put small objects of interest, such as a small car or coloured ball, inside the shakers so that your child can open them and find out what is making the noise.

> REMEMBER TO PUT SMALL OBJECTS OUT OF REACH OF CHILDREN WHEN THEY ARE NOT BEING SUPERVISED.

Early Listening: Awareness of Sound
SOUND PLAY

Some sounds may be easier to hear than others. Children may have difficulty hearing bells, but will respond to the noise of a drum. If your child has a hearing loss, this game may help you find out which particular sounds he can hear best.

Have a box of noisy toys hidden away. These could include:

Drum	Mouth organ	Xylophone
Whistle	Squeaky toy	Castanets
Party horn	Bells	Tambourine

1 Allow time for your child to explore and play with different sounds.

2 Choose a toy which you think your child may be able to hear. When your child is not looking, make a noise and see if he responds. If your child turns to the sound, let him have the toy to play with.

3 Another time, see if your child will respond in a particular way when you make a sound; for example, he could post a brick into a hole in a box when you ring the bell.

Write down any sounds you think your child responds to during the day for example: telephone, doorbell, whistling, banging.

SOUNDS MY CHILD RESPONDS TO

Date	Sound

Early Listening: Awareness of Sound
SOUND/NO SOUND

❑ *Exploring sound and silence*

As your child's listening skills improve, he will learn to tell the difference between sound and silence. It is important for your child to explore things which are silent as well as things which are noisy. A collection of both noisy and silent toys could include:

◆ a rattle,
◆ a teddy or glove puppet,
◆ a squeaky toy,
◆ a rag doll or other soft toy,
◆ an alarm clock (clocks which vibrate are available for deaf children).

Take toys out of a box one at a time, and let your child play with them. Draw your child's attention to things which are noisy and those which do not make a sound, using gesture or sign to help if necessary.

A glove puppet could:

◆ play with a rattle very quietly or bang and shake it to make a noise;
◆ go to sleep and wake up when the alarm clock rings/vibrates.

❑ *Sound shakers*

You will need four small tins with lids, and a few small objects to put inside.

1 Put a small object in two of the tins and leave the other two empty.

2 Shake one of the tins and see if your child can tell you if it makes a noise or not. You may need to use sign or gesture.

3 Give the tin to your child to shake, and let him open it to see if there is anything inside.

Learning to tell the difference between sound and silence will help children to learn that sound exists. Games which encourage children to listen for a sound and respond to it will be useful for all children who need to develop their listening skills.

Jack-in-the-box

Let your child climb into a large cardboard box or laundry basket. Bang on a drum or an old biscuit tin and show him how to jump up like a jack-in-the-box when you make the noise. Your child may need to see you making the sound to start with, and may need some encouragement to wait for the next sound before jumping up again. Start with a loud sound, and gradually use quieter and quieter sounds for your child to listen to.

Come out of the house

Make a large box into a house with cut-out windows and a door, or use a playhouse. Make a sound for your child to listen to from inside the house. When he hears the sound, he could come out through the door.

Stepping stones

Use cushions or small boxes to make stepping stones across the room. Choose a sound for your child to listen to, such as a drum beat or a whistle. Every time you make a sound, your child should jump to the next stepping stone.

Follow the footsteps

Make several pairs of cardboard feet, and make a trail around the room. Every time you make a sound, your child should put a foot on one footprint, so that he slowly moves across the footsteps from one end of the room to another.

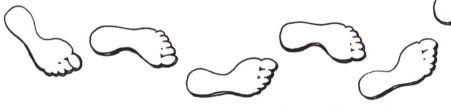

The four games above will work well with pairs of children, when one can make the sound and the other carry out the actions.

Early Listening:
Awareness of Sound
STOP/START

These games may work well with groups of children.

❑ **Soldiers**

1 March around the room together, banging a drum or an empty tin. When you stop making a noise, stop marching, and stand up straight like a soldier.

2 Once your child has got the idea, just bang the drum and let him do the marching!

3 Finally, keep the drum out of his sight, so that he is listening rather than watching.

❑ **Listening to music**

Play some music on a tape recorder or music centre and let your child listen to it. Your child may also like to feel the vibrations of the music by putting his hands on the speakers or by sitting on a hard surface next to the speakers. Dance a doll or teddy to the music and make it fall down when the music stops.

Dance or rock to the music and encourage your child to do the same until the music stops. Alternatively, your child could sit on a cushion, pretend to go to sleep or put on a hat when the music stops.

❑ **Pass the bean bag**

A group of children can pass a bean bag round. When the music stops, the child holding the bean bag has to perform an action, such as putting on a hat or scarf, walking round the circle with the bean bag on his head, or throwing the bean bag into a bucket.

P

Early Listening: Awareness of Sound
LOCATING SOUNDS

Helping children to find where the sound is coming from will be important for safety. For example, it may be useful for locating the sound of a car coming or a warning beep. It will also be a useful skill for identifying where speakers are in a group.

Locating sound may be difficult for some children with a hearing loss, but can be improved, particularly if the hearing loss is similar in both ears.

❏ Hide and seek the sound

Choose a toy which your child can hear. It may be a loud banging toy or a quiet musical toy. Show this to your child and let him play with it for a while. Explain that you are going to hide yourself in the room with the toy. He may need to see you doing this at first. Make the sound from your hiding place, and see if he can find you by listening for the sound.

❏ Blind man's buff

Demonstrate to your child the noise you are going to make. Then blindfold your child and make the sound on one side of his head. See if he can point to the ear in which he heard the sound.

❏ Find the musical toy

Wind up the musical toy and listen to the sound together. Put a cushion at each end of the settee and hide the toy underneath one of them. Encourage your child to listen and locate the sound. Instead of cushions, you could use tins or boxes to hide the toy in.

For a louder sound, you could use a small tape recorder and some music. For a quieter sound, try an alarm clock beeping.

As your child gets better at this game, hide toys anywhere in the room.

Early Listening:
Awareness of Sound
RECORD CARD

Child's name: ....

Before children can understand the complex sounds of speech and language, they need to develop an awareness of sounds around them.

AIM OF ACTIVITIES	COMMENT AND DATE
EXPLORING SOUND (p40). To provide experience of different sounds and vibrations.	
Activities tried:	
SOUND PLAY (p41). To encourage and identify response to a variety of sounds.	
Activities tried:	
STOP/START (p44). To recognize when a sound stops.	
Activities tried:	
LOCATING SOUNDS (p45). To identify the direction of sound.	
Activities tried:	

P

EARLY LISTENING: AWARENESS OF VOICE

SECTION 4

Early Listening: Awareness of Voice

General points

What is meant by 'awareness of voice' and why is it important?

Children learn a lot about voice and speech sounds before they recognize the meaning of words. Listening games encourage children to develop a greater awareness of speech sounds and early words, through listening and responding in a particular way.

How can awareness of voice be improved?

Make funny sounds for your child to listen to and vary the pitch of your voice when you talk, to make it more interesting to listen to. Exaggerate facial expression, and make use of all the senses of hearing, touch and vision.

All young children learn through repetition. Singing simple rhymes and songs over and over again will help your child to become more aware of voice and rhythm of speech.

Symbolic sounds are speech sounds which are used to represent objects in a meaningful way, in this case the movement of vehicles and the noises animals make. They are repetitive, so provide plenty of practice.

❑ Vehicle sounds

Beep beep (car)   Na-na (ambulance/fire engine)
Choo choo (train)

Choose a toy to play with, and make the sound that goes with it, for example, 'choo choo' for the train. Use the sounds in sentences, not just on their own.

Push a train along the table or floor, saying "Choo choo".

Push it towards a box with a hole in it and stop using your voice as it disappears into the hole.

Push the train round a track, and say, "Choo choo" as it goes through a tunnel.

❑ Animal sounds

Woof woof   Quack quack
Moo   Baa

Choose any animal sound to work on, preferably one which your child is most interested in. Use the animal noises frequently when playing, but remember to talk in sentences as well as making the noises on their own.

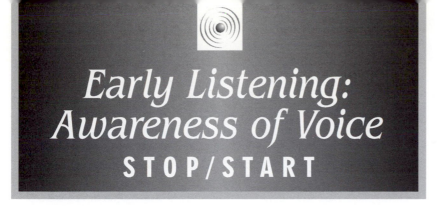

Early Listening: Awareness of Voice
STOP/START

❑ *Stop/start games*

Choose one of the sounds, such as ahhhh.
Choose a toy, such as the car.
Push the car along the table, using your voice to make the sound. When you stop the car, stop making the sound.

Variations

Draw a line on the paper when you make a sound.

Your child could walk round the room when you use your voice.

❑ *The Grand Old Duke of York*

Your child could march round the room to the song, 'The Grand Old Duke of York', and stand still when you stop. You don't always have to sing to the end. Stop halfway through if your child knows the song well, and then carry on.

You will need:

a car, *or*
wind-up toy, *or*
pencil and paper.

Sounds to make:

ahhhhhh
oooooo
ayyyyyy

S E C T I O N 4

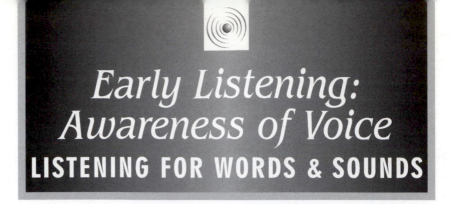

Early Listening: Awareness of Voice
LISTENING FOR WORDS & SOUNDS

An early hearing test used in many clinics is called the 'Go Test'. The child listens for the word, 'Go' and responds in a particular way, for example by throwing a brick in a box. This is a game enjoyed by many children and encourages them to wait, listen and respond to sounds. It can help pinpoint speech sounds which your child is having difficulty hearing.

You will need:

toy people and a car/bus, *or* cotton reels and a box, *or* pegs and a peg board, *or* rings to put on a stick.

❏ Listening for 'GO'

Give your child one object, for example, a cotton reel.
Show him how to throw it in a box when you say 'Go'.
Every time you say 'Go', he should throw a cotton reel into the box.
At first use a loud voice and let your child see your face.
Once he understands the game, use a quieter voice, and

cover your mouth so that he is listening rather than looking.

❏ Listening for vowel and consonant sounds

Try the same game with different sounds. Your child may find consonant sounds more difficult to hear than vowel sounds.

Vowel sounds: ar   oo   ow   ee
Consonant sounds: b   g   ch   m   d   sh   s

Early Listening: Awareness of Voice
LISTENING FOR WORDS IN A PHRASE

❑ *Ready, steady, GO*

Children may be encouraged to wait and listen for the word 'Go' in the following games.

- ◆ Roll cars or balls to and fro.
- ◆ Knock down a tower.
- ◆ Push a toy person down a slide.
- ◆ Roll a ball down a slide.
- ◆ Make pop-up toys jump up.
- ◆ Run races.

❑ *One, two, three and ... JUMP*

- ◆ Jump off a small step.
- ◆ Jump into a 'pretend' puddle (this could be a plastic hoop).
- ◆ Make toys jump.

❑ *One, two, three and ... UP*

- ◆ Lift your child up.
- ◆ Throw a ball up high.
- ◆ Curl up small and slowly stretch up high.

❑ *One, two, three ... FALL DOWN*

- ◆ Make Humpty Dumpty fall down.
- ◆ Make a tower of bricks fall down.
- ◆ Make a teddy fall down.

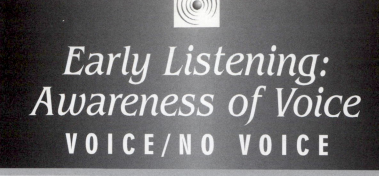

Early Listening: Awareness of Voice
VOICE/NO VOICE

These games help children discriminate between spoken words and silence. Children respond in a particular way by carrying out an action when you use your voice to give the command. If a lip pattern only is used, without voice, children do not carry out the action.

❑ Actions

Clap hands.
Turn around.
Curl up small.

Play a game of 'Simon says' with or without voice.

1 Choose one of the above actions to start with; for example, 'turn around'.

2 Say, "Simon says, 'Turn around'", using a sign or gesture if necessary, and help your child to turn round.

3 This time, use a lip pattern, but no voice, when you say, "Turn around". Your child should stay still when you use no voice.

❑ Names

Choose an action, such as 'clap hands'.

Say your child's name and show him how to clap his hands.

Using lip patterns only, say his name again; this time, he should not clap: he should only clap when you use your voice to call his name.

It may be useful to play these games with a small group of children, where they can learn from each other.

❑ Listening for early words

Your child could carry out an action associated with a particular word, depending on whether you use voice or just a lip pattern. He could carry out any of the following.

Drive a car into a garage, or blow a horn every time you say, 'car'.

Shake a rattle when you use your voice to say, 'baby'.

Put a sticker on a cardboard cut-out shoe when you use your voice to say, 'shoe'.

Put an apple in a shopping basket when you use your voice to say, 'apple'.

Put a cut-out cardboard jumper on a washing line when you use your voice to say, 'jumper'.

Drop a boat in the water when you use your voice to say, 'boat'.

Early Listening: Awareness of Voice
NURSERY RHYMES

Children can listen for speech sounds before they understand the words.

❑ *Nursery rhymes*

1 Humpty Dumpty sat on a wall
Humpty Dumpty had a great FALL...

When children hear 'FALL', they can:

make a toy Humpty fall off a wall;
fall off a chair onto a large bean bag or cushion;
bang a cymbal or a saucepan lid.

2 The Jack-in-the-box jumps UP like this
He makes me laugh as I waggle his head
I gently press him DOWN again
Saying, "Jack-in-the-box you must go to bed."

Children can do the actions for 'UP' and 'DOWN' or make a Jack-in-the-box pop up and down.

3 Ring-a-ring-o'roses
A pocket full of posies
Atishoo, atishoo
We all fall DOWN

Children walk round in a circle and have to listen for the last word of this song before falling down at the end.

4 Ten fat sausages sizzling in a pan,
One went POP and the other went BANG!

Children clap hands when they hear 'POP' and 'BANG'.

SECTION 4

Early Listening: Awareness of Voice

RECORD SHEET

Child's name: ....

Listening for voice sounds develops an awareness of speech sounds and early words.

AIM OF ACTIVITIES	COMMENT AND DATE
SYMBOLIC SOUNDS (p50). To develop awareness that speech sounds can represent objects in a meaningful way.	
Activities tried:	
STOP/START (p51). To recognize when voice stops.	
Activities tried:	
LISTENING FOR WORDS & SOUNDS (p52). To develop the ability to respond to specific words and sounds.	
Activities tried:	

Early Listening:
Awareness of Voice
RECORD SHEET

AIM OF ACTIVITIES	COMMENT AND DATE
LISTENING FOR WORDS IN A PHRASE (p53). To develop the ability to anticipate and respond to specific words and sounds.	
Activities tried:	
VOICE/NO VOICE (p54). To discriminate between spoken words and silence.	
Activities tried:	
NURSERY RHYMES (p55). To anticipate words in a familiar repetitive rhyme.	
Activities tried:	

S E C T I O N 4

VOCALIZATIONS

Vocalizations

General points

Why is it important to encourage babble and vocalizations?

Before children learn to speak, they need to experiment with different sounds which will help develop control over the movements of the mouth and tongue necessary for speech. Vocal play is a way of exploring how to make different sounds, and is an important stage in learning to speak. Early vocalizations are mostly vowel sounds; for example, ee/oo. Consonant sounds soon appear and babbling becomes tuneful: 'ba ba ba mama'. If a hearing loss is present, babbling may stop if the child cannot hear the sounds he is making. If the child wears hearing aids, the babbling may start again, but may need to be actively encouraged.

How can vocalizations be encouraged?

◆ Singing, talking and laughing are all enjoyable and will encourage your child to be vocal. Sit your child on your lap facing you and bounce him up and down. Sing songs and rhymes and play tickling games.

◆ Whenever your child makes a noise, try to respond to it (within reason!) by either repeating the noise or extending it into a word.

◆ Children are often most vocal when they are excited or amused. Use these times to encourage vocalizations and babble.

◆ Make your voice more interesting by letting it go up and down and loud and soft, or make funny sounds for your child to copy.

◆ Give your child time to vocalize. Wait a moment before repeating a funny noise or a game your child enjoys.

◆ When your child makes a noise, reward him by giving attention and praise, or surprise him by using a hidden pop-up or wind-up toy.

◆ Make a note of any new sound your child makes and write the date so that you can see progress.

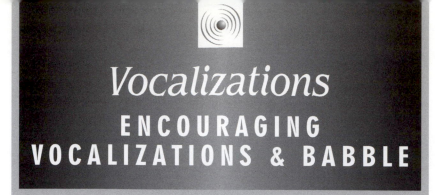

Vocalizations
ENCOURAGING VOCALIZATIONS & BABBLE

Make appropriate noises when playing with toy animals or cars and encourage your child to join in. At this stage it does not matter if the noises your child makes do not sound like words.

❏ *Symbolic sounds*

Use sounds for appropriate feelings and situations. For example:

'ahhhhhh'	– Poor teddy, he's hurt.
	– What a lovely baby!
'ooooooh'	– I wonder what's in here?
	– Isn't that smart?
'mmmmmm'	– Lovely ice cream!
	– That's my favourite.

❏ *Musical blowers*

You may use paper horns, whistles, mouth organs, recorders, or anything else which makes a sound. If your child can hear these sounds, he will probably want to have a go. Young children may not have the breath control to make the noise, but, in trying, are quite likely to vocalize instead.

❏ *Trumpets*

Use an old toilet roll or kitchen roll tube as a 'pretend' trumpet to make noises through.

❏ *Echo mike*

'Echo mikes' can be useful for encouraging children to use their voices by making noises or singing into the microphone. They are not expensive and can be bought from toy shops or catalogues.

❏ *Telephone play*

Talk or babble into the telephone and encourage your child to copy you. Provide him with opportunities to play with the telephone alone too.

Make a toy telephone with two old yoghurt pots and string to encourage a two-way 'conversation'.

❑ *Glove puppets*

These can be a useful way of encouraging children to vocalize.

◆ Play tickling games, or 'Round and round the garden' games.

◆ Make the puppet sing and clap.

◆ Give the puppet a kiss.

◆ Stroke the puppet.

◆ Give it a drink and make it say, 'Thank you'.

◆ Give the puppet a hat (the puppet could drop it, put it on upside down, put it on your head).

◆ Make the puppet hide, and then say, 'Boo!'

◆ Plays 'wake up' and 'go to sleep' games (your child has to make a noise to wake the puppet up).

Vocalizations
LIP & TONGUE GAMES

These games encourage lip and tongue movements. Practice with lip shapes and tongue movements will strengthen the muscles used in speech. This will be important for the development of early vocalizations and babble.

❑ *Lip games*

- ◆ Push lips forward to make kissing shapes.
- ◆ Put lipstick on and make round prints on paper.
- ◆ Alternate kissing shapes with smiling shapes.
- ◆ Blow instruments.
- ◆ Play blow football with straws.
- ◆ Blow out candles, saying 'p'.
- ◆ Looking in the mirror, say 'oo' followed by 'ee'. Then say 'sh' followed by 's'.

❑ *Tongue games*

- ◆ Look in the mirror and encourage your child to copy you sticking your tongue in different positions:
    upwards,
    downwards,
    sideways,
    round,
    to touch your nose.

- ◆ Lick lollies, sticky paper, stamps, stars, envelopes.
- ◆ Coat the back of a spoon with sticky food and then lick it clean.
- ◆ Put something sweet on your child's top lip (chocolate or jam) and encourage him to lick it off with his tongue.
- ◆ Use the *Mr Tongue Story* (see *Resources and Materials* at the end of this book).

Vocalizations
SOUNDS MY CHILD MAKES

Make a note of any new sounds your child makes, and write the date.

Date	Sound

Vocalizations
RECORD SHEET

Child's name: ....

Vocal play is a way of exploring how to make different sounds and is an important stage in learning to speak.

AIM OF ACTIVITIES	COMMENT AND DATE
ENCOURAGING VOCALIZATIONS & BABBLE (p62). To encourage the use of voice in a meaningful way.	
Activities tried:	
LIP GAMES (p64). To develop familiarity with lip shapes.	
Activities tried:	
TONGUE GAMES (p64). To develop familiarity with the use and position of the tongue.	
Activities tried:	
SOUNDS MY CHILD MAKES (p65). To record the range of sounds made over a period of time.	
Sounds made:	

AUDITORY DISCRIMINATION

SECTION 6

Auditory Discrimination

General points

What is meant by 'auditory discrimination'?

Auditory discrimination games build on children's listening skills by developing a greater awareness of small differences between sounds. Through these games, children can learn to discriminate between one sound and another. Games in this section aim to develop discrimination skills by listening to a range of sounds.

Why is it important to improve auditory discrimination?

In listening for small differences between sounds, children learn to distinguish between differences in pitch (high/low), differences in volume (loud/quiet), differences in length of sound (long/short) and differences in rhythm (fast/slow). Learning to recognize these differences will be useful for understanding spoken language, and can also encourage communication through music and movement.

How can auditory discrimination be improved?

In addition to specific games, drawing children's attention to sounds in the environment and talking about them can help children notice the differences between sounds, such as loud and quiet/high and low.

❏ *Copying musical rhythms*

Fast and slow

Make fast or slow beats on a drum or a tin, and encourage your child to copy you. Let him see what you are doing to start with. If he understands the difference between fast and slow, make the sound from behind a screen or behind a chair, so that he is listening, rather than looking for the difference.

Long and short

Make long and short sounds with a mouth organ, whistle or paper horn. Party horns are useful for *seeing* the length of sound. Otherwise, the sound of a whistle may be felt as well as heard. Encourage your child to listen for the difference between long and short sounds, and copy you.

Loud and quiet

Make loud sounds by banging two cymbals or saucepan lids together and encourage your child to do the same. Then make very quiet sounds and see if your child can copy you. Exaggerate your movements to emphasize the difference. When your child has got the idea, make the sounds from out of his view and see if he can copy.

Rhythms

Older children may be able to copy simple rhythms, for example, slow–fast–fast–slow. Again, let your child see first, and then hide the instrument, and encourage your child to copy the rhythm by listening alone.

High and low

Make a low sound on a piano, xylophone or chime bar and encourage your child to copy it. Do the same with a high sound and talk about the differences. Turn your child round or show him how to cover his eyes. See if he can copy the next sound you make without looking.

Auditory Discrimination
MOVEMENT

Most of these games are more suitable for groups or whole classes of children, rather than individuals.

❑ *Fast and slow*

Children can run fast like a hare and crawl slowly like a tortoise when there is a change in the sound signal, such as a fast drum beat and a slow drum beat.

❑ *Long and short*

Children can take long strides like a giant when they hear a long sound from a cymbal, or short steps like a mouse when they hear short taps.

❑ *Loud and quiet*

Children can stamp their feet loudly when they hear a loud banging on wooden sticks, or tiptoe very quietly around the room when the banging is quiet. Or they can jump when they hear a loud noise and sit down when they hear a quiet nose.

❑ *Rhythms*

Children in a circle can each have a sound maker, such as a pair of coconut shells. They do not all have to have the same. They pass a sound round the circle, starting with a single beat and trying to keep the rhythm going. As they improve, more difficult rhythms can be introduced.

❑ *High and low*

When you make a high sound such as sleigh bells, children can stretch up high, and when you make a low sound like a drum beat, they can curl up into a ball.

Auditory Discrimination

❏ Traffic lights

Red: Stop (bang tambourine once)
Amber: Get Ready (drum fingers on tambourine)
Green: Go! (shake tambourine)

Work on 'Stop' and 'Go' to start with. When you shake the tambourine, children should walk or run round the room pretending to drive a car. When you bang the tambourine once, children should freeze. Now introduce the sound for 'Get Ready'. Children should jog on the spot when you drum your fingers on the tambourine. Thus amber means jog on the spot, green means run round the room and red means stop and freeze.

❏ Hunt the bear

One child can 'hunt the teddy bear' which has been hidden in the room. Other children play loudly on their sound makers when the 'hunter' is close to the bear, and quietly when he is far away.

❏ Find a hat

Children can walk round the room to one rhythm and find a hat to put on when the beat changes.

❏ Pass the sound

Each child needs a sound maker. Children sit in a circle with their sound maker. The first child makes a sound and the second child has his turn only when the first sound is finished. Some sounds will be short (a bang on a drum) and others will be longer (a bang on a cymbal).

Auditory Discrimination
MATCHING SOUNDS

Start by choosing two different sounds to work on. Give your child time to experiment with making different sounds. Then you can copy the sounds that he makes and take turns.

Hide the sound makers behind a screen and make the noise. When your child hears the noise, see if he can match and copy it. To make this game harder, use three different sound makers.

You will need:

things to bang: tin lids
or plant pot and stick;
things to shake: tins
with cottons reels inside
or bunches of keys;
things to scrape:
comb and ruler
or corrugated cardboard
and pencil.

❏ Matching sounds to actions

You will need three different sound makers: such as a bell, a squeaky toy and a whistle.

Your child could respond to different sounds in a particular way. For example, he could turn around on hearing the bell, touch his head on hearing the squeaky toy, or fold his arms on hearing the whistle.

When your child is familiar with the game, make the sounds from behind a screen so that he has to listen carefully.

Auditory Discrimination
TAPED SOUNDS

You will need:

a tape recorder;
sound toys, such as
a drum, a squeaky toy
or a musical toy.

❑ ***Noisy toys***

Choose two or three noisy toys that your child enjoys playing with. Tape their noises one at a time and let your child listen to them. Put the toys in front of your child and see if he can match the sounds on the tape to the toys.

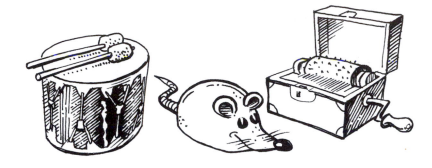

❑ ***Body sounds***

Encourage your child to copy simple body sounds, for example:
    clapping hands,
    tapping three fingers on one hand,
    stamping feet,
    slapping knees,
    clicking the tongue,
    popping the cheeks.

Tape these noises one at a time and listen to them. See if your child can recognize the sounds on the tape and join in with them.

❑ ***Household sounds***

Make your own listening tape by taping sounds you hear around the house, such as the telephone ringing, a door banging, the washing machine, the baby crying.

❑ ***Sound lotto***

Match sounds to pictures and talk about them.

Auditory Discrimination
RECORD SHEET

Child's name: ....

Auditory discrimination of sound aims to build on basic listening skills by encouraging a greater awareness of small differences between sounds.

AIM OF ACTIVITIES	COMMENT AND DATE
COPYING SOUNDS (p70). To listen to and remember differences between sounds.	
Activities tried:	
MOVEMENT (p71). To respond appropriately to different sounds.	
Activities tried:	
MATCHING SOUNDS (p73). To identify and match or respond to different sounds.	
Activities tried:	
TAPED SOUNDS (p74). To identify subtle differences between taped sounds.	
Activities tried:	

SPEECH
DISCRIMINATION

SPEECH DISCRIMINATION
INTRODUCTION

Many of the activities in this section are particularly relevant for hearing impaired or phonologically disordered children, who frequently have difficulties with speech perception and production. Activities need to be worked through in a systematic order, and will need careful supervision and guidance from the professionals concerned.

Syllable discrimination

Resource pictures are included for specific work on syllable discrimination. Vocabulary should be familiar to the child if possible, and may be chosen from the syllable lists on page 87. The following combination of syllables is in increasing order of difficulty and should be worked through at the child's own pace:

1 a one-syllable word versus a four-syllable word;

2 a one-syllable word versus a three-syllable word;

3 a one-syllable word versus a two-syllable word;

4 discrimination between three words instead of two, which will take this one step further: for example a one-syllable, a two-syllable and a three-syllable word.

A variety of vocabulary and activities can be used to maintain children's interest and motivation.

Vowel discrimination

Children learn to associate abstract sounds with concrete pictures, and then begin to discriminate between a variety of long vowel sounds:

Long vowel sounds:	*Associated pictures:*
oo (ʊ)	wind
or (ɔ)	oar of boat
ah (ɑ)	crocodile
er (ɜ)	teddy thinking
ee (i)	mouse

For children with a hearing loss, it is important that these vowel sounds are presented in syllable or word contrasts, such as moo/more; bee/baa; purr/paw.

Children can also listen for differences between long and short vowels:

Short vowel sounds:	*Corresponding pictures:*
a (æ)	ant
o (ɒ)	kangaroo hopping
i (ɪ)	robot
u (ʌ)	rocket
e (ɛ)	frog

The vowel cards referred to in these activities are available from The Nuffield Dyspraxia Programme (address in *Resources and Materials* section).

Minimal pairs

Minimal pairs are useful for developing vowel discrimination. They use contrasting vowels and diphthongs within meaningful words:

(a) *Long versus long vowels*

key	car
boot	Burt
sea	saw
pea	paw

(b) *Long versus short vowels*

cart	cat
sheep	ship
sleep	slip
heart	hat

(c) *Short versus short vowels*

cat	cot
dig	dog

(d) *Diphthongs*

boy	bye
pear	pie
boy	bow

(e) *Vowels versus diphthongs*

cat	kite
cart	coat
bat	boat

Pictures can be photocopied from the resource pictures at the end of this section.

Speech Discrimination

General points

What is meant by 'speech discrimination' and why is it important?

'Speech discrimination' activities encourage children to listen for differences between two or more speech sounds or words and phrases, building on the listening skills they already have. Recognizing small differences between speech sounds is an important step in learning to understand spoken language.

How can speech discrimination be improved?

Children can learn to recognize differences in the length, rhythm and intonation of sounds, words and phrases. In the early stages, visual clues such as facial expression, gesture, signs and lip patterns will help children learn the difference between two contrasting sounds.

Offering choices will give children everyday practice in listening for differences between sounds in a natural environment. For example, if your child wants a toy, you could ask whether he wants the 'car' or the 'aeroplane', rather than giving him what you think he wants straight away.

Children with hearing losses may always need some help from lip reading to discriminate between certain speech sounds, but their listening skills can often be improved considerably with practice, by making the best use of residual hearing.

Discrimination between long and short sounds or phrases

Children can be 'trained' to hear the difference between long and short sounds or phrases. Learning to recognize differences in length and duration of sound will help them become more aware of the sounds in running speech, helping them to make sense of spoken language.

Discrimination between familiar sounds and words

Pairs of words are chosen by taking into account their contrasting visual and auditory pattern. For example 'moo' and 'quack quack' sound very different and also look very different on the lips. Gradually, a greater range of sounds is introduced so that children are discriminating between three or four similar sounds. As they become more familiar with different sounds, they may begin to discriminate by listening alone.

Syllable discrimination

Learning to recognize differences in pitch, rhythm and intonation of speech is essential for the understanding of spoken language. Syllable discrimination activities aim to make children more aware of these differences.

Vowel sounds

Vowel sounds occur in every spoken word. Children learn in a structured way to hear the difference or recognize different lip patterns associated with different vowel sounds. Learning to recognize these differences will give them useful information about sounds within words.

Minimal pairs

These are words for example, 'chip' and 'chop', which differ in only one sound. Only the vowel sound is different. With training, children learn to recognize the difference between these vowel sounds, through listening or lip reading.

❏ Long and short sounds

Long sounds: ahhhhhhhhhh (aeroplane)
Short sounds: b–b–b (boat)

Play with a collection of toy boats or aeroplanes or draw some pictures and introduce the sounds. Encourage your child to make the sounds while he plays.

Make a scene of the sea and the sky on a big sheet of paper or blackboard. When you say, "ahhhhhh", show your child how to put an aeroplane in the sky. When you say, "b–b–b", he could put a boat in the sea.

❏ Other long and short sounds

Long sounds: ooooooooooo (wind)
Short sounds: p–p–p (fish)

Stick clouds in the sky for 'oooooo' and fish in the sea for, 'p–p–p'.

❏ Long and short phrases

Long phrases:	Short phrases:
Turn around	Run
Ready, steady, go	Stop
Clap your hands	Jump
Run to the door	Up
Put your hands on your head	Clap

Choose one of the above pairs, for example, 'Run' and 'Turn around'. Give one of these commands and show your child what to do, using signs, gestures and demonstration if necessary. With practice, your child will learn to discriminate between the two commands and carry out the appropriate action without help.

Speech Discrimination
FAMILIAR SOUNDS & WORDS

❑ Animal sounds

miaow   quack quack
moo   woof woof
baa   cluck cluck

Choose two animal sounds which look and sound very different, for example, 'miaow' and 'quack quack'. Play with the animals and make the noises when appropriate.

Draw a picture of a cat and stick it on one of the boxes. Draw a picture of a duck and stick it on the other box.

When you say, "Miaow", your child could put a brick into the box with the picture of the cat on it. When you say, "Quack quack", he should put a brick in the other box.

Play similar games with other pairs of animal sounds. You could collect pictures of milk for a cow every time you say, "Moo" and pictures of a bone for a dog when you say, "Woof woof".

❑ Transport sounds

choo choo (train)   beep beep (car)
brummm (motorbike)   whee (aeroplane)

You could do the same with pairs of transport sounds, hiding toys or pictures of vehicles around the room. When you say, "Choo choo", ask your child to look for the trains. When you say, "Brummm", your child should find the motorbikes.

You will need:

toy farm animals;
two old boxes or pots;
bricks.

SECTION 7

a spinning top:
'round and round';
a drum/hammer:
'bang bang';
a drawstring bag.

❏ Action sounds

Play with the toys, making the appropriate noises as you play. When your child is familiar with the different sounds, hide the toys and put one of them into the bag. Make the noise associated with that toy and see if your child can guess what is inside before he has a look. Use pictures for your child to point to if he is unable to say the words.

For other action sounds, you will need:

a toy ladder: 'up up up';
a toy slide: 'down down down';
a plastic jumping frog: 'jump jump';
a walking wind-up toy: 'walk walk'.

❏ Names

This game will help your child become more familiar with the names of family and friends. Using very similar names will make the game more difficult.

Wrap up some small sweets or small toys and write a name on each one. Let your child help you choose two or three names for the small parcels. Mix them all up and put them in a box or bag. Take out one at a time and call out the name. Let your child give the sweet or toy to the right person.

Speech Discrimination
SYLLABLE LIST

One-syllable words	Two-syllable words	Three-syllable words	Four-syllable words
cow	monkey	elephant	caterpillar
dog	rabbit	butterfly	rhinoceros
bird	tiger	kangaroo	alligator
cake	apple	banana	cauliflower
pear	biscuit	tomato	
jam	ice cream	potato	
milk	carrot	strawberry	
car	lorry	aeroplane	helicopter
bus	taxi	motorbike	
train	digger	bicycle	
house	window	telephone	television
bed	table	computer	washing machine
chair	chimney	radio	record platyer
ball	teddy	roundabout	Jack-in-the-box
book	baby	telephone	jigsaw puzzle
doll	balloon	umbrella	
box	basket	rocking horse	
hat	jumper	pyjamas	wellington boots
shoes	trousers	cardigan	swimming costume
dress	slippers	dressing gown	

You will need:

pairs of model animals
or pictures

❑ Animals

Choose two contrasting animal words; for example:

bird (one syllable) and caterpillar (four syllables)

These words look and sound very different. When your child is familiar with the words, share the animals between you and play a pairs game. Ask your child for one animal to make a pair with yours and see if he can find the correct one. Use pictures or signs to help at first.

Choose different pairs of animal words to make this more difficult, and gradually introduce a third word; for example:

cow (one syllable) and elephant (three syllables)

dog (one syllable) and bird (one syllable)

bird (one syllable), rabbit (two syllables) and butterfly (three syllables)

❑ Food

Choose two contrasting words, for example:

cake (one syllable) and banana (three syllables)

Draw large pictures of a cake and a banana. When you say one of the words, your child could stick a star or sticker onto the correct picture.

Try to use the words in a sentence: 'Put a star on the banana' *or* 'Put a star on the cake'.

You will need:

two empty shoe boxes
bricks
pictures of two vehicles

❑ Transport

Choose two words from different syllable lists, for example:

car (one syllable) and helicopter (four syllables)

Stick one picture on each shoe box. Your child should put a brick in the correct box, according to which word you say. Use sentences rather than single words.

Alternatively, your child could post pictures into post boxes.

❑ The house

Choose two words from different syllable lists; for example:

house (one syllable) and television (four syllables)

Find three or four pictures of each word you have chosen. Stick the paper clips onto the cardboard pictures so that they can be picked up by the magnet.

When your child hears a word, he can pick up the correct picture by using the 'fishing rod'.

You will need:

pictures of furniture stuck onto card

paper clips

a 'fishing rod' made from a magnet attached to a piece of string

❑ Objects

Choose two contrasting words; for example:

ball (one syllable) and telephone (three syllables)

Draw a simple picture of a ladder on each sheet of paper. At the top of each draw a picture of the words you have chosen.

Put a counter or a toy person at the bottom of each ladder. Depending on which word you use, your child can make the person jump up the ladder one step at a time. When the person is at the top of the ladder, give your child the real toy to play with as a reward.

You will need:

two sheets of paper
pencil and crayons
two toy people
or two counters

❑ Clothes

Choose two words to start with, from different syllable lists; for example:

hat (one syllable) and wellington boots (four syllables)

Depending on which word you say, your child could stick that item of clothing on one of the mannequins.

Alternatively, he could colour it in or hang it on a 'washing line'.

You will need:

cardboard cut-outs of boys and girls with clothes to put on

You will need:

picture vowel cards
two empty pots
beads or bricks

ahhhhh

❏ **Long vowel sounds**

Each vowel card represents a different sound; for example:

ahhhhh   ooooooo   eeeeeeee

(crocodile)   (wind)   (mouse)

Choose two sounds to start with, for example 'ahhhhh' and 'eeeeeeee'. Show your child pictures of crocodiles and mice, and stick a different picture on each empty pot.

When you say, "ahhhhh", your child should throw a bead or brick into the pot with the crocodile picture on it. When you see "eeeeeee", he should put a bead or brick into the pot with the mouse picture on it.

You will need:

picture vowel cards
crayons
stickers

❏ **Long vowel sounds versus short vowel sounds**

Long vowels	Short vowels
ahhhhh (crocodile)	a (ant)
oooooo (wind)	o (kangaroo)
eeeeeee (mouse)	i (robot)
	u (rocket)
	e (frog)

Choose two sounds to work on, one from each list for example:

'ahhhh' (long vowel) and 'e' (short vowel)

(crocodile)   (frog)

ahhhhh

Stick pictures of crocodiles and frogs round the room. When you say, "ahhhhhh", your child could get a picture of a crocodile and colour it or put a sticker on it. When you say "e", he could find a picture of a frog.

Put the sounds into sentences where possible.

Speech Discrimination
MINIMAL PAIRS

Minimal pairs are pairs of words which only differ in one sound. In this list, only the vowel sounds are different, so your child must learn to listen or watch for the difference between these sounds:

key versus **car**
ship versus **sheep**
chip versus **chop**
boy versus **bye**

Choose one pair of words to work on for example:

ship and sheep

Put the two sticks on the table. Put the picture of the ship next to one stick, and the picture of the sheep next to the other.

When you say "ship", help your child to put a bead on the correct stick. Do the same for "sheep". Continue until all the beads are on the sticks.

You will need:

minimal pairs pictures
two stacking rings, or
two beads-on-a-stick games

SECTION 7

Speech Discrimination
SONGS & STORIES

❑ **Action rhymes**

Action rhymes such as 'The wheels on the bus' may be sung fast or slow and children join in with either fast or slow actions. Songs may also be sung loudly or quietly.

❑ **Stories**

When reading a favourite story, encourage your child to listen out for certain words. For example:

Goldilocks and the Three Bears

Every time you say, "Goldilocks" in the story, your child could shake some bells, and when you say "bear", your child could roar, or take a teddy out of a box.

Three Little Pigs

Every time you say the word "pig", your child could make a squeaky toy squeak, and when he hears "wolf", he could blow down a paper cut-out of a house.

Three Billy Goats Gruff

Every time your child hears "trip trap", he could stamp his feet, and when he hears "out jumped the troll" he could make a glove puppet jump up.

Gingerbread Man

When your child hears "Run, run as fast as you can", he could make a cardboard cut-out of a gingerbread man run, and when he hears "Stop, little gingerbread man", he could clap his hands or hold up a STOP sign.

These listening games can be played with one or two children.

Speech Discrimination
RECORD SHEET

Child's name: ....

Speech discrimination aims to build on basic listening skills already acquired, thus improving a child's comprehension of spoken language.

AIM OF ACTIVITIES	COMMENT AND DATE
LONG & SHORT SOUNDS & PHRASES (p84). To discriminate between two long and short sounds or phrases.	
Activities tried:	
FAMILIAR SOUNDS & WORDS (p85). To discriminate between two or more contrasting sounds or words.	
Activities tried:	
SYLLABLE DISCRIMINATION (p87). To discriminate between two or more words, differing in number of syllables.	
Activities tried:	

Speech Discrimination
RECORD SHEET

AIM OF ACTIVITIES	COMMENT AND DATE
VOWEL SOUNDS (p90). To discriminate between contrasting vowel sounds.	
Activities tried:	
MINIMAL PAIRS (p91). To discriminate between vowels within pairs of words.	
Activities tried:	
SONGS & STORIES (p92). To listen for and anticipate words within connected speech.	
Activities tried:	

Speech Discrimination
MINIMAL PAIRS
PICTURES

Speech Discrimination

MINIMAL PAIRS
PICTURES

Early Communication Skills

© *Charlotte Lynch & Julia Kidd, 1999*
You may photocopy this page for administrative use only

Speech Discrimination
SYLLABLE
PICTURES

S
E
C
T
I
O
N

7

© Charlotte Lynch & Julia Kidd, 1999
You may photocopy this page for administrative use only

Speech Discrimination

SYLLABLE
PICTURES

P

Speech Discrimination
PICTURES

Speech Discrimination
PICTURES

Speech Discrimination
PICTURES

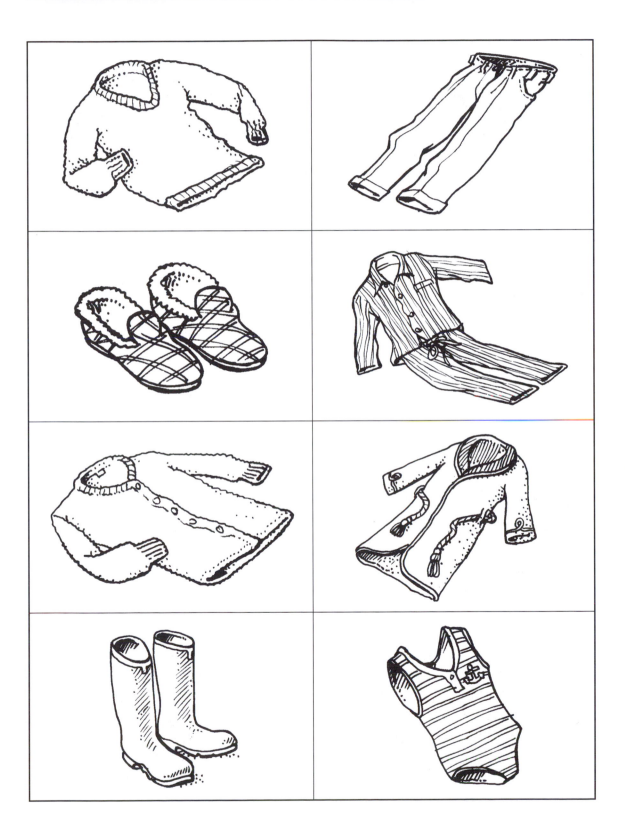

AUDITORY/ VISUAL MEMORY

SECTION 8

Auditory/Visual Memory

General points

What is 'auditory/visual memory'?

An essential part of language learning involves remembering information which is taken in through the auditory and visual channels (through the ears and eyes). Some children find it difficult to process and remember what they have heard and seen.

Why is auditory/visual memory important?

Improving memory is important for future language learning. Children use all their senses to take in information about language. Organizing and remembering this information is necessary for the sequencing of ideas and thoughts when using language.

How can auditory/visual memory be improved?

Auditory/visual memory games aim to improve memory for spoken language through listening and looking. These games will encourage your child to take in and recall information. In many of the games, the skills of auditory, visual and sequential memory overlap.

You will need:

between two and seven different toys, such as a car, a doll, a teddy, a ball, a book and a cup

❏ Kim's game

Choose two or three of the toys and play with them. Put the toys on a table free from other distractions. Cover your child's eyes or show him how to turn around while you take one of the toys away.

See if your child notices which toy is missing. To help him understand, you could say, 'Where's Teddy? Teddy's gone!' and pretend to look for it. Then make a big fuss about finding the teddy and putting it back on the table.

As your child gains in confidence, gradually increase the number of toys you use to make the game more difficult, or hide more than one toy at a time.

You will need:

two to five different-sized coloured barrels; two to five miniature toy animals

❏ Animal hide and seek

Start with two or three barrels and the same number of toy animals. Give your child one animal at a time and show him how to hide them inside the barrels. Drawing simple pictures can help remind your child where each one has been hidden. Before opening the barrels again, see if your child can remember which animal is inside each one. Give clues if necessary: perhaps a sign or the animal noise.

Gradually increase the number of animals you hide to make the game more difficult.

Auditory/Visual Memory
MATCHING PICTURES

❑ Snap

Share out the cards so that you both have five of the same picture. Put your child's set facing upwards in front of him. Show him three of your pictures and line them up on the table. Help your child to find the three pictures to match yours.

Repeat the game. To make it harder, turn your pictures upside down and see if your child can match them from memory.

Gradually add more pictures.

❑ Matching pairs

Memory games can be played using only a few pairs of cards to start with. See how many pairs your child can find by turning over two at a time.

❑ Shopping game

Choose five picture cards and put them on the table. Say or sign which three pictures you want him to find for your shopping basket: for example, "Give me the jelly, the sausages and the apple." Accept them in any order to start with. Then encourage your child to present the pictures in the order in which you asked for them: (1) jelly, (2) sausages, (3) apple. You may need to repeat the sequence several times.

For a variation of this game, you could write a shopping list, using words and pictures as an aid to memory.

You will need:

a set of Snap cards

You will need:

Snap cards or pictures of food; a shopping basket

SECTION 8

Auditory/Visual Memory
GROUP GAMES

These games can be played with two or more children or adults.

❑ Who's got the animal?

You will need:

three to six different pictures, such as a cow, a pig and a horse

Let your child give everyone a picture. Talk about it: for example, "Daddy's got the cow – Moo!" Each person could mime their own picture to make it more memorable.

Turn each card face down and see if your child can remember who has which picture, asking for example, "Who's got the cow?" Alternatively, mix the pictures up and ask your child to return them to the correct person.

Gradually add more pictures, so that each person has two or three.

❑ Changing places

You will need:

an item of clothing for each child, such as a hat, gloves, sunglasses, a scarf

A small group of children should sit on chairs in a circle. Give each child an item of clothing. Talk about what each child is wearing. Encourage each child to remember his own item of clothing and put it under his chair.

Call out the names of two articles of clothing. The two children to whom they belong should put on their item of clothing and swap places. To make it harder, call out more names of clothes. To finish with, put all clothes in the middle of the circle, and see if children can remember which item belongs to whom.

Auditory/Visual Memory
SEQUENCING

❑ *I went for a walk*

Start the game off by choosing one of the toy animals (a duck, for example). Say, "I went for a walk and I saw a duck." Encourage your child to repeat the word or sign for 'duck'.

Line up another animal behind the first one (a tortoise, for example) and say, "I went for a walk and I saw a duck and a … tortoise."

Encourage your child to repeat 'duck' and 'tortoise' or make the appropriate signs.

Add another animal (a cat, for example) and say, "I went for a walk and I saw a duck, a tortoise and … a cat."

Put a screen in front of the animals and see if your child can remember them all in the correct order. Gradually increase the number of animals you use.

❑ *I went shopping*

Put the box of toys in the middle of a small circle of children. The first child should choose one toy from the box and show it to everyone. He should then hide it under his chair. He could say, "I went shopping and I bought …" The next child has to remember the first toy and repeat what the first child said; then choose another toy, hide it under his chair, adding it to what he has just said. The third child has to remember the last two toys and choose the next one. And so on.

You will need:

miniature toy animals and a screen (an old box or book)

You will need:

a box of toys

S
E
C
T
I
O
N

8

You will need:

three noisy toys or musical instruments, such as:
a plastic cup and spoon *or* a triangle to bang/hit;
a paper horn *or* a recorder to blow;
a money box with coins *or* a tambourine to shake

❑ Sequencing sounds

Make a sound using one the above toys, and encourage your child to do the same. Then make a sequence of two different sounds and encourage your child to copy both sounds in the correct order. If your child is coping with these activities, make a sequence of three sounds and help him repeat all three sounds in the correct order.

To start with, let your child see you making the different sounds.

❑ Sequencing actions

Make a series of different actions and encourage your child to copy your actions in the same order. Start with a sequence of two and gradually introduce new actions; for example: shake your hands in the air; hide your hands behind your back; put your hands on your hips.

❑ Sequencing everyday events

Draw simple pictures of everyday actions, for example:

◆ *washing clothes*: dirty clothes in a basket, a washing machine, clothes hanging on the line, ironing;

◆ *making cakes or biscuits*: ingredients, the mixture in the bowl, in the baking tray, in the oven, on the wire rack and so on;

◆ *sequences in nature*: a bird making a nest, eggs in the nest, eggs beginning to crack, mummy bird bringing a worm for the babies.

Talk to your child about each picture. Then cut the pictures out, muddle them up and ask your child to help you rearrange them in the correct order.

❏ *Sequencing stories*

Look at picture books, or read favourite stories over and over again. Repetitive stories are popular amongst young children. Suitable stories may include: 'The Gingerbread Man', 'Goldlilocks and the Three Bears', 'The Three Little Pigs' and 'Three Billy Goats Gruff'.

As your child becomes familiar with the story, encourage him to anticipate what will happen next before turning over the page.

Draw simple pictures of the story. Muddle the pictures up and ask your child to help you rearrange them in the correct order. If you can get hold of old books, pictures can be cut out. You may try making stick puppets of the characters in the book to act the story out.

SECTION 8

Child's name: ....

An essential part of language learning involves remembering information which is taken in through the auditory and visual channels.

AIM OF ACTIVITIES	COMMENT AND DATE
VISUAL (p112). To develop visual memory skills: Kim's game, Animal hide and seek, Memory game, Matching pairs, Snap, Changing places, Who's got the animal?	
Activities tried:	
SEQUENTIAL (p115). To develop sequential memory skills: I went for a walk, I went shopping, Sequencing sounds and actions/everyday events/stories.	
Activities tried:	
AUDITORY. To develop auditory memory skills: Shopping game, Who's got the animal?, Changing places.	
Activities tried:	

EARLY WORDS

SECTION 9

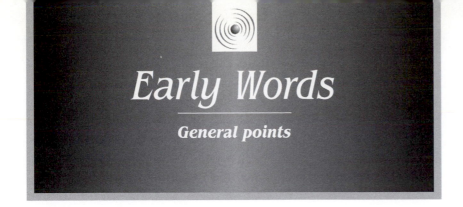

Early Words

General points

Early words are learnt through copying and repetition. Children need to hear a word many times and in many different situations before they fully understand its meaning. They will understand more than they can say to begin with.

The 'List of Early Words' consists of a few of the most commonly learnt first words. Most of them are important and useful words for communication in the early years. There will be other words which individual children find interesting or useful, and these should also be encouraged. Most words are best learnt through spontaneous use during everyday events. Additional games can be played to reinforce understanding of these words.

Hints for encouraging early words

◆ Choose one or two words to focus on for a week, a month or as long as is necessary for your child. Choose words which your child will find useful or interesting. They may be words which your child is already trying to say.

◆ These words can be used repetitively, and in many different ways. The words should be used in short, simple sentences wherever possible, not on their own.

◆ Use the words in everyday situations wherever possible.

◆ Give your child time to talk. Copy or extend any words he attempts and praise all efforts.

◆ Make sure that family and friends are aware of the words you are trying to encourage, so that they can help too.

◆ It is important not to spoil your child's enjoyment of a game by insisting on an attempt at the word.

Early Words
LIST OF EARLY WORDS

Familiar names	Common objects	Social words	Action words
Mummy	car	hello	go
Daddy	ball	bye bye	fall
own name	book	please	up
man	dog	thank you	stop
boy	cat	more	walk
baby	bird	no	push
	fish	again	pull
	shoe		wash
	bag		drink
	apple		round and round
	cup		

Describing words	Pronouns	Symbolic words
big	me	beep beep
small	mine	choo choo
hot	you	quack quack
cold	yours	moo
wet		bang

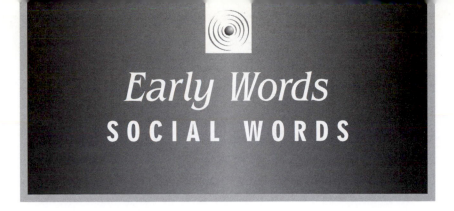

Early Words
SOCIAL WORDS

❑ ***Hello/bye bye***

Toy telephone: talk into the receiver, saying "Hello" or "Bye bye".

Glove puppets: make the puppets wave 'Hello' and 'Bye bye'.

Peepo games: hiding and reappearing.

Mirror play: looking in the mirror, and saying "Hello" and "Bye bye".

Play shops: saying "Hello" and "Bye bye" when the customer arrives and leaves.

❑ ***More***

Playdough, food and drink: give a little at a time, so that your child is likely to ask for more.

Bubbles: encourage your child to say, "More" before blowing bubbles again.

Building towers: giving your child one brick at a time, and wait for an attempt at 'more' before giving him the next one.

Beach ball or balloon: blow them up a little at a time; stop and allow your child time to ask for 'more' before continuing.

Money box: Give your child one coin at a time to put in the money box.

❑ ***No***

Knocking coloured balls into holes: pretend to get it wrong (put the wrong colours in the holes).

Inset puzzles or posting boxes: try the same activity again. "Will it fit in there? No, I don't think so. What about this one? No!"

Hiding games: hide a small object in one hand. Your child should guess which hand it is in.

Lift-the-flap books: as you are lifting the flaps say, "Is it Spot the dog? No, it's the lion."

❑ ***Again***

If your child is amused by something you do, and wants you to repeat it, encourage him to say, "Again" before you do it. Try some of the following activities to get your child's interest:

pop-up ball,
wind-up toy,
building and knocking down towers,
tickling games,
letting air burst out of a balloon.

WHOOSH

S E C T I O N 9

❑ *(All) gone*

Emphasize the word, 'gone', whenever the toys disappear:

Post toys into a box with a hole in the top.

Cover objects with a scarf or hide them under a pot.

Hide finger puppets behind your back.

Roll a ball across the table and into a tin.

❑ *Up*

Encourage the use of 'up' in everyday situations: up the stairs/steps; lifting your child up.

Toy slide or ladder and a person: make the person move up a step every time you or your child says, "Up".

Pop-up rocket: encourage an attempt at 'up' before your child presses the button.

Jack-in-the-box: there are opportunities for both 'up' and 'down' with this toy.

Copying games: standing up/sitting down, arms up/arms down.

Rhymes: Roly poly, roly poly, up up up.

❑ *Stop*

Watch out for when the music and movement of these toys stop:

> toy record player,
>
> maypole,
>
> wind-up musical toy,
>
> wind-up toy,
>
> cars.

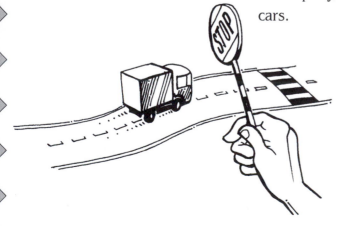

Make a STOP sign and play a game of stopping traffic at pedestrian crossings/ traffic lights/junctions and so on.

P

❑ *Round and round*

Say "Round and round" with the movement of toys such as a roundabout, a spinning top or a music box.

Drawing circles round and round the page.

Play hospitals, putting on bandages, round and round the arm, leg or head.

Use rhymes: 'Round and round the garden, like a teddy bear'; 'The wheels on the bus go round and round'.

❑ *Go*

Say "Go" before you:

    roll a ball down a tube or to each other,

    release toys,

    push a toy man down a slide,

    knock down a tower.

Early Words
DESCRIBING WORDS

❑ *Hot/cold*

Everyday activities provide opportunities for use of the words 'hot' and 'cold': making jelly, ice cubes and ice lollies; warnings about hot water, tea, dinner or radiators.

❑ *Wet*

There are many everyday opportunities for using the word 'wet':

water play,
washing teddy's clothes,
hanging out the washing,
spilling a drink,
splashing in puddles.

❑ *Big/small*

Sort big or small balls, animals or cars into boxes or large hoops.

Stories such as 'Goldilocks and the Three Bears' and the 'Three Billy Goats Gruff' are useful for talking about big and little.

Cut out three different sized arches in an old box: big, medium and small. Roll marbles across the table into the arches.

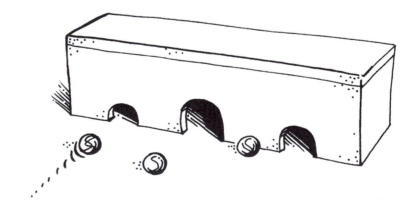

REMEMBER TO KEEP SMALL MARBLES OUT OF REACH OF VERY YOUNG CHILDREN.

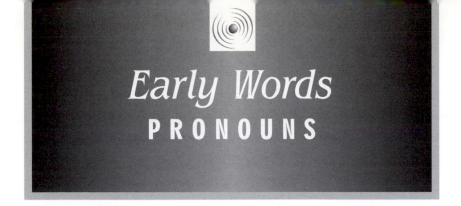

Early Words
PRONOUNS

❑ ***Mine/yours***

Snap cards: share cards using appropriate vocabulary, such as this is yours/mine.

Lotto games: match the cards and talk about who each card belongs to: 'Is this yours? No, it's mine.'

Share toys or sweets.

Tea party with tea set: give out and match different colour cups and saucers.

Thread beads: each person can choose a different colour to make a necklace: 'That's mine, it's a red one; here's a blue one, this is yours.'

❑ ***My turn/your turn***

Take turns to:

> throw a bean bag into a bucket,
> knock down skittles,
> colour part of a picture,
> throw a dice,
> make a plastic frog jump into a 'pond'.

❑ ***Bang***

Bang pegs/balls into holes.

Bang two bricks together.

Bang a drum.

❑ ***Beep beep***

Push a car along the table or floor.

Make the car disappear into a hole in a box.

Hide the car under a beaker and push it along.

Make a paper road for cars to travel on.

Push the car along your child's arm/into your pocket/up your sleeve.

❑ ***Quack quack***

Play with plastic ducks in the water.

Make a cardboard duck on a stick puppet and make it pop up from under a table.

Make duck shadow puppets.

Feed the ducks.

Rhyme: 'Five little ducks went swimming one day'.

Early Words
FAMILIAR NAMES

❑ *Mummy, Daddy and own name*

Turn-taking games: throwing a ball, blowing bubbles, sharing sweets or fruit.

Magazine pictures: find pictures of Mummy, Daddy and a child, and then sort them into different boxes.

Photographs: take photographs of family and close friends and stick them into a book, writing the name underneath. Look at the book frequently, and say the names.

Toy people and dolls: match them to pictures or members of the family, ie mum, dad, grandma, baby.

Glove or finger puppets: play with man, lady, boy and girl puppets or draw faces on your fingers.

Make a lift-the-flap house and draw people looking out of the windows.

Draw a picture of a bus/tractor/car and cut out faces from old photographs to stick in the driver's seat.

❑ *Man*

Put men in a bus or car: give your child one man at a time.

Hide toy people in pots or tins.

Put a man on top of a tower.

Hide a man in one of your hands.

SECTION 9

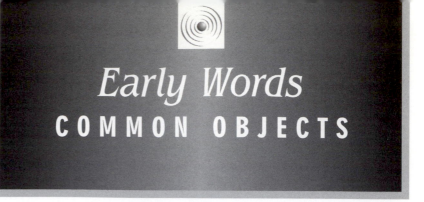
❏ **Car**

Playing with cars in different ways will provide many opportunities for using the word:

Create a toy garage (a simple one can be made by cutting out doors from an old box and colouring or painting it).

Sort cars into colours, sizes and shapes.

Make a car from *Lego*® bricks.

Cut out magazine pictures of cars.

Roll cars down a slope or through a cardboard tube.

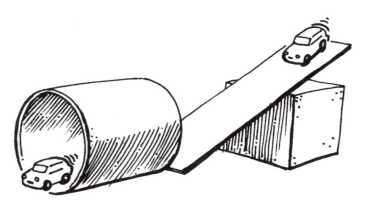

❏ **Ball**

Blow up a beach ball.

Play with skittles and a ball.

Make *Plasticine*/playdough balls.

Blow table tennis balls.

Roll balls to and fro.

Draw, colour and cut out pictures of balls.

Hide balls around the room.

Early Words
RECORD SHEET

Child's name: ....

Word/s chosen:...

DATE	GAME	IMITATION OF WORD (when your child copied you)	SPONTANEOUS USE OF WORD (when your child used the word on his own)	RESPONSE (what you said)

© Charlotte Lynch & Julia Kidd, 1999
You may photocopy this page for administrative use only

Early Words
RECORD SHEET

Child's name: ....

Children need to hear a word many times and in many different situations before they can begin to understand and use early words spontaneously.

AIM OF ACTIVITIES	COMMENT AND DATE
To develop comprehension. To encourage imitation of gestures and sounds. To use sounds in a meaningful way. To develop use of meaningful words. To record progress of emerging words and developing vocabulary.	
SOCIAL WORDS (p123). hello, bye bye, more, no, again.	
Activities/words tried:	
ACTION WORDS (p124). (all) gone, up, stop, round and round, go.	
Activities/words tried:	
DESCRIBING WORDS (p126). hot, cold, wet, big, small.	
Activities/words tried:	

Early Words
RECORD SHEET

AIM OF ACTIVITIES	COMMENT AND DATE
PRONOUNS (p127). mine, yours, my turn, your turn. Activities/words tried:	
SYMBOLIC WORDS (p128). bang, beep beep, quack quack. Activities/words tried:	
FAMILIAR NAMES (p129). Mummy, Daddy, own name, man. Activities/words tried:	
COMMON OBJECTS (p130). car, ball. Activities/words tried:	

RESOURCES & MATERIALS

Resources & Materials

Sound-sensitive toys

Dancing cola cans and flowers which move when you make a sound are available in the high street. These can be used to encourage vocalizations. Other sound-sensitive toys such as toy crabs and spiders are available from:

Fun and Achievement
76 Barracks Road
Sandy Lane Industrial Estate
Stourport-on-Severn
Worcestershire DY13 90B

Echo mikes can be purchased cheaply from high street stores or children's party catalogues. Sounds are amplified with an echo effect.

Vibrating toys

The Vibrobubble is also available from the Fun and Achievement catalogue (see above). This vibrates and makes various sounds when buttons are pressed, raising awareness of sound. Some also have flashing lights.

Vibrating alarm clocks (not toys) can be purchased from:

Sound Advantage plc
1 Metro Centre
Welbeck Way
Peterborough
PE2 0UH

Speech viewer

This computer program has some uses for encouraging vocalizations, speech sounds and suprasegmental work on pitch and volume. There are some lovely graphics as feedback and reinforcement. Available from:

Papworth Ability Services (UK) Ltd.
11 Langley Business Court
World's End
Beedon
Nr. Newbury
Berkshire RG20 8RY

Musical instruments

A wide range of quality instruments suitable for use with severely and profoundly deaf children, including wooden tone bars, bass drums and a variety of more unusual instruments, are available from:

Music Education Supplies Limited
101 Banstead Road South
Sutton
Surrey SM2 5LH
Tel 0181-770 3866

For those who wish to extend their use of music with deaf children, it may be worth applying to 'The Beethoven Fund' for a grant to purchase musical instruments (donations to schools only, not to individual children). Apply to:

Beethoven Fund for Deaf Children
2 Queensmead
St John's Wood Park
London NW8 6RE
Tel 0171-586 8107

Many of the songs and rhymes in this book can be found in: Karen King, Oranges and Lemons, Oxford University Press, 1985, and This Little Puffin, Nursery Songs and Rhymes, Penguin, Harmondsworth, 1969.

Mr Tongue Story

This is a story about Mr Tongue who does different things, encouraging the child to copy tongue movements in an enjoyable way. This is available for 50p, inclusive of post and packaging from:

Dudley Priority Health NHS Trust
Speech Centre
Central Clinic
Hall Street
Dudley
West Midlands DT2 7BX
Tel 01384 459530 ext. 207 or 205

Vowel cards

Vowel cards mentioned in the activity sheets can be obtained from:

Speech Therapy Department
Nuffield Hearing and Speech Centre
Grays Inn Road
London WC1X 8DA

APPENDIX

FURTHER READING

Connery V *et al, Nuffield Centre Dyspraxia Programme,* Nuffield Hearing and Speech Centre, London, 1985.

Cooke, J, Early Sensory Skills, Winslow Press/Speechmark, Bicester, 1996.

Cooke J & Williams D, Working with Children's Language, Winslow Press/Speechmark, Bicester, 1988.

Cooper Jean, Moodley M & Reynell J, Helping language development, Edward Arnold, London, 1978.

Crystal D, Listen to your child; A parent's guide to child language, Penguin, Harmondsworth, 1986.

Jeffree D & McConkey R, Let me Speak, Souvenir Press, London, 1976.

Ling D, Speech of the Hearing Impaired Child. Theory and Practice, The Alexander Graham Bell Association for the Deaf, Washington, 1976.

Locke A, Living Language, NFER–Nelson, Windsor, 1985.

McConkey R & Price P, Let's Talk – Learning Language in Everyday Settings, Souvenir Press, London, 1986.

McCracken W & Sutherland H, Deaf Ability, Not Disability: a guide for parents of hearing impaired children, Multilingual Matters Ltd, Clevedon, 1991.

Williams D, Early Listening Skills, Winslow Press/Speechmark, Bicester, 1996.